£3·50

C000084505

DATE DUE

14 NOV 2007

YORK NOTES

Z for Zachariah

Robert O'Brien

Notes by Paul Beadle

Longman   York Press

YORK PRESS
322 Old Brompton Road, London SW5 9JH

ADDISON WESLEY LONGMAN LIMITED
Edinburgh Gate, Harlow,
Essex CM20 2JE, United Kingdom
Associated companies, branches and representatives throughout the world

First published 1998

ISBN 0–582–36846–4

Designed by Vicki Pacey, Trojan Horse, London
Illustrated by Jonathan Edwards
Phototypeset by Gem Graphics, Trenance, Mawgan Porth, Cornwall
Colour reproduction and film output by Spectrum Colour
Produced by Addison Wesley Longman China Limited, Hong Kong

CONTENTS

PREFACE

York Notes are designed to give you a broader perspective on works of literature studied at GCSE and equivalent levels. We have carried out extensive research into the needs of the modern literature student prior to publishing this new edition. Our research showed that no existing series fully met students' requirements. Rather than present a single authoritative approach, we have provided alternative viewpoints, empowering students to reach their own interpretations of the text. York Notes provide a close examination of the work and include biographical and historical background, summaries, glossaries, analyses of characters, themes, structure and language, cultural connections and literary terms.

If you look at the Contents page you will see the structure for the series. However, there's no need to read from the beginning to the end as you would with a novel, play, poem or short story. Use the Notes in the way that suits you. Our aim is to help you with your understanding of the work, not to dictate how you should learn.

York Notes are written by English teachers and examiners, with an expert knowledge of the subject. They show you how to succeed in coursework and examination assignments, guiding you through the text and offering practical advice. Questions and comments will extend, test and reinforce your knowledge. Attractive colour design and illustrations improve clarity and understanding, making these Notes easy to use and handy for quick reference.

York Notes are ideal for:
• Essay writing
• Exam preparation
• Class discussion

The author of these Notes is Paul Beadle, who teachers English and Drama in a comprehensive school in the North-East of England. He is a senior examiner for one of the United Kingdom's largest GCSE examination bodies.

The text used in these Notes is the Harper Collins Lions edition, first published 1976.

Health Warning: **This study guide will enhance your understanding, but should not replace the reading of the original text and/or study in class.**

PART ONE

INTRODUCTION

HOW TO STUDY A NOVEL

You have bought this book because you wanted to study a novel on your own. This may supplement classwork.

- You will need to read the novel several times. Start by reading it quickly for pleasure, then read it slowly and carefully. Further readings will generate new ideas and help you to memorise the details of the story.
- Make careful notes on themes, plot and characters of the novel. The plot will change some of the characters. Who changes?
- The novel may not present events chronologically. Does the novel you are reading begin at the beginning of the story or does it contain flashbacks and a muddled time sequence? Can you think why?
- How is the story told? Is it narrated by one of the characters or by an all-seeing ('omniscient') narrator?
- Does the same person tell the story all the way through? Or do we see the events through the minds and feelings of a number of different people.
- Which characters does the narrator like? Which characters do you like or dislike? Do your sympathies change during the course of the book? Why? When?
- Any piece of writing (including your notes and essays) is the result of thousands of choices. No book had to be written in just one way: the author could have chosen other words, other phrases, other characters, other events. How could the author of your novel have written the story differently? If events were recounted by a minor character how would this change the novel?

Studying on your own requires self-discipline and a carefully thought-out work plan in order to be effective. Good luck.

Robert C. O'Brien was the pseudonym of Robert Leslie Conly, who was born in New York City in 1922, one of a family of seven. He died in 1973, not long after *Z for Zachariah* had been published in the USA.

Youth

In his youth, Robert O'Brien had intended to become a professional pianist, but when he finished high school he took on a variety of jobs, including work in a mail room, a bookshop, and an advertising agency. His literary career probably had its beginnings when he was a student working in camps for boys during the summer vacations; here he would tell stories, sitting by night around the campfire or in the cabin. He realised this was excellent training for finding out what types of story young people like.

Writing

He worked on a newspaper as a reporter for a while, then as a re-write man for a news agency, a staff writer for various magazines, and a freelance writer of stories, poems and essays. He then took up a post on the staff of *National Geographic* magazine in Washington, DC. He became an editor for the magazine and spent the last twenty-two years of his life with this internationally famous publication which deals with scientific, geographic and ecological matters – subjects which are at the heart of *Z for Zachariah* (1974) and his other novels, *The Silver Crown* (1968), *Mrs Frisby and the Rats of NIMH* (1971) and *Report from Group 17* (1972).

C̲ONTEXT & SETTING

Z for Zachariah is essentially a science-fiction novel, based on the fear, which was very real in the 1970s when the book was written, that nuclear war was certainly possible and, indeed, probable.

Political context

The end of the Second World War, when atomic bombs were dropped on the Japanese cities of

Hiroshima and Nagasaki, had proved how horrific the potential of nuclear power was when used in aggressive situations. After the war, from the 1940s onwards, there was a tension between some of the victors. The United States of America and the Union of Soviet Socialist Republics (USSR) had been allies in the fight against Japan and Hitler's Germany, but they were ideologically very far apart – the USA was a capitalist nation, while the USSR favoured communism. There developed between the two countries a situation known as the Cold War, in which fear of one another's ideologies and intentions led to mounting strain on their relationship.

Z for Zachariah is set in the United States after a nuclear war. The circumstances of the war are never alluded to – in fact, before Loomis arrives, Ann is even unsure of what kind of warfare had been employed – and it is not stated which other country was involved in this war with the USA. However, its consequences have been devastating.

The political situation which resulted in this terrible and sudden war are of little importance to the author. The fact that a war has occurred, and that the American (or even global) population has been destroyed, is the starting point of a novel which explores the essence of what it is to be human, the point of existence itself.

Science fiction To categorise the novel as being part of the genre we generally call science fiction is perhaps a little misleading, although the best quality science fiction does address universal issues like those in *Z for Zachariah*. The novel is not, though, about aliens, robots, other planets or bizarre technology. It is written in diary form – the diary of a fifteen-year-old girl (she celebrates her sixteenth birthday half way through the novel) named Ann Burden. At the beginning of the

story, Ann believes that she may be the only person left
alive on the planet.

Geography   Ann has lived all her life on a farm in an area called
Burden Valley, named after her long-established family
who were the first settlers there. By some freak of
nature, the valley has remained free from radiation
pollution and is still capable of sustaining life. The
valley seems to have been protected by the high
surrounding hills. Claypole Ridge is fifteen miles to the
north. Ten miles beyond this is the nearest settlement,
Ogdentown, which she knows from having gone to
school there. She also knows, from her family's
explorations, that 'there is no one left alive in
Ogdentown'. Near her homestead, Burden Farm, there
is Burden Hill, six miles away, some woodland, and a
cave; there are also two streams and a pond. In the
valley itself there is a church, and a store which was
owned by Mr and Mrs Klein. This store had served
the Burdens, and an Amish (see Glossary on p. 15 of
these Notes) community who had farms just to the
south of the valley. There is a highway nearby which
led to Dean Town, which Ann describes as 'a real
city – twenty thousand people, much bigger than
Ogdentown'. Ann had hoped to go to study at the
Teachers' College in Dean Town, but she now knows
there is no one left alive there, or in the Amish
settlement.

This, then, is the apparently desperate situation in
which we find Ann Burden at the beginning of the
novel. She had lived with her family: father, mother,
brother Joseph and cousin David. They, together with
the Kleins, had gone to search for signs of life to the
south, but they never returned. She was left alone, until
Mr Loomis appears on the scene.

PART TWO

Summaries

General summary

Chapters
1–5:
A stranger
arrives

A nuclear holocaust has taken place and fifteen-year-old Ann Burden believes herself to be the sole survivor – the valley in which she lives has somehow escaped the devastation. Ann's parents, brother, and cousin, and the only other people in the valley, the Kleins, who ran the store, had gone to search for signs of life, but never returned. Ann has been living by herself for over a year, when she sees, with a mixture of hope and fear, a column of smoke in the distance, gradually coming nearer.

Leaving behind no trace of her existence, Ann cautiously decides to move to a cave further up the hill, from where she watches a man approaching, who is dressed in an orange plastic suit and is pulling a wagon. Obviously amazed and relieved to find a green, living valley, the stranger checks for radiation and removes his mask.

The following day, he mistakenly bathes in the contaminated Burden Creek, rather than in the pure stream that Ann has been using as a water supply. Soon after this, Faro, cousin David's dog, who had run off some time ago, returns. Moving between the cave and house, Ann fears Faro may give her presence away.

The man goes looking around the valley, but becomes ill and drags himself to his tent. When he does not emerge, Ann goes to see what has happened. He has become very ill indeed, but comes around enough to tell her he has contracted radiation sickness. In his delirious sleep he keeps mentioning 'Edward'.

Chapters
6–10:
Nursing the
sick

Ann nurses the man and finds out that his name is John R. Loomis. Before the nuclear war, he was working on a type of plastic which would keep out radiation – the suit he was wearing, which is the only one of its kind, and the cover of the wagon are made out of this material. Loomis has scientific and mechanical knowledge which will surely be of help to Ann, but at the same time he displays a quirky and aggressive nature, especially when Ann enquires about Edward. He also continues to talk in his sleep in a worrying manner.

Despite this, Ann even begins to innocently consider the prospect of marriage to Loomis. Then he becomes seriously ill again. She continues to nurse him, but on her return home after doing some chores she sees Loomis stagger from the house, take his gun, and shoot at the top of the building. She calms him and puts him back to bed, but his nightmares return and Ann finds out that Loomis shot Edward because he tried to take the suit from the laboratory where they worked.

Chapters
11–15:
Living with a
murderer

Loomis is so ill he nearly dies. Ann goes to the church with Faro to pray for both Loomis and herself. While at the church, Faro finds a baby crow which has fallen from its nest, and Ann leaves it outside for its parents to find. Later she finds it gone, and is certain it has been returned to its nest. Ann looks on this as a good omen, and sure enough Loomis begins to get better, and Ann begins to think optimistically. Ann loves books and considers the possibility of going to Ogdentown to get some, using the suit; but this is clouded by the thought of what happened to Edward. Ann also dismantles the stove and brings it to the house. She is able to roast a chicken and bake a cake for her sixteenth birthday.

Chapters
16–20:
Attacked and
hunted

Ann's optimism is marred by Loomis's attitude. As he gets better he becomes more domineering. Then, one night, Loomis grabs her hand and makes what Ann calls a 'pass' at her. She is afraid and disturbed and realises that Loomis is trying to take control of her.

Loomis demands that she read and play the piano for him but this makes her feel tense. The next night he creeps into her room and attempts to rape her. She escapes and runs to the cave.

Ann realises that Faro is a threat to her, and Loomis makes a point of putting the dog on a leash and tying it up. She decides to go to talk to Loomis to work out a compromise. Ann keeps her hiding place at the cave secret. Loomis tries to find out where she is staying. She realises she can never trust him again. He does not even mention the attempted rape.

Ann still milks the cows and collects vegetables, ensuring that she gives Loomis exactly the same amounts as herself. Loomis, however, is training Faro to track, and he is learning how to drive the tractor. Ann begins to wish Loomis had never come to the valley, and she begins to think about escape.

Chapters
21–26:
Leaving the
valley

For about ten days the system Ann has worked out seems to be satisfactory. But Loomis is plotting. Ann finds Loomis has taken the tractor key and she goes to ask him for it. He does not give it to her, and again tries to ascertain her whereabouts and persuade her to return to the house. Ann refuses to tell him and leaves. A little later Loomis searches the store to see if she is staying there and puts padlocks on the doors.

Ann decides to go to the house to confront him. He shoots her in the ankle. Ann runs for her life. Loomis tracks her, using Faro, and Ann decides to shoot the dog to safeguard her own safety, but she cannot go through with it. Loomis gives up searching, but not before he has found Ann's cave and destroyed all her property.

Ann hides like a hunted animal for over a month. She decides she must steal the safe-suit and leave the valley.

One day she sees the door to the store has been left open but when she goes towards it Loomis shoots at her, and she realises she has walked into a trap. Ann flees, but Loomis trails after her with Faro on the leash. Ann fires above Loomis's head and scares him off. Faro has leapt into the contaminated Burden Creek and dies shortly afterwards.

This sparks Ann into action. She manages to take the cart, put on the suit, and head out of the valley, but she feels a need to speak to Loomis one last time.

Loomis comes after her. Ann is hidden, and as Loomis gets down from the tractor, Ann could easily shoot him, but does not. Loomis demands the safe-suit and pleads with her to stay, but Ann turns away and walks out of the valley, leaving it to him. Loomis yells after her that he has seen birds to the west. She acknowledges this, and walks on in hope.

DETAILED SUMMARIES

CHAPTERS 1–5: A STRANGER ARRIVES

CHAPTER 1

May 20th

Ann is afraid. She has seen a column of smoke rise into the air on three consecutive days, first behind Claypole Ridge (fifteen miles away), and gradually moving nearer. The last time she saw smoke it was a giant cloud, the result of the nuclear holocaust last year which left her alone on Burden Farm. She fears whoever it is that is approaching and her first thought is to go to the church and pray.

We learn that there is no one left alive in Ogdentown (ten miles further on from Claypole Ridge), something that Ann knows because her father, her brother Joseph and her cousin David had gone there after the war ended, and found only dead bodies.

May 21st

What is the significance of Ann's certainty that the approaching stranger is male?

The smoke is coming closer, and Ann realises the approaching stranger is deciding whether to take the east-west highway, which leads to Dean Town, or Country road 793, which leads over the ridge to Burden Valley. She wants him to follow the highway, to stay away, but she knows that if he gets to the top of the ridge he will see the green trees of the valley and come in her direction, since all else is dead.

Ann begins to explain why she is writing this document, which she began in February: she had started to forget when, and even whether, things had happened; in addition, the diary was 'like having someone to talk to' (p. 8), since she had thought she was the only person left in the world.

Is Ann's caution justified?

Ann tells of how at first she hated being alone. One by one, the radio stations had stopped transmitting, and the final broadcasts she had heard had disturbed her. The man had broken down and cried on air, and this has made her cautious: anyone who did arrive could be mad or mean or a murderer, so she has decided not to show herself immediately to anyone who arrives. Consequently, she has started to move her possessions to the cave.

May 22nd

The smoke has risen again from the same place as yesterday, and Ann knows that the person or persons have camped at the crossroads and are exploring east and west – she fears the next step will be to explore south, towards her valley.

Meanwhile, Ann tells us that on the day after the trip to Ogdentown her family, along with Mr and Mrs Klein, had travelled southwards towards the Amish community to see how they had fared; then they were to travel on to Baylor and Dean Town. No one returned, and Ann realises that the Amish have all perished, as has everyone in Dean Town. She has also climbed the trees on the hills which surround the valley, and beyond the valley there is no sign of life – sensibly she does not go out there.

COMMENT   The diary form of the novel is immediately apparent in the dates of the entries. This means that the story is told as a **first-person narrative** (see Literary Terms) and we see all the events through Ann's eyes.

The first two sentences are short and shocking, pulling us straight into Ann's predicament: 'I am afraid. Someone is coming' (p. 5). This is a technique Robert O'Brien uses to great effect throughout the novel.

Another comparable technique is the use of **flashbacks** (see Literary Terms). This is effective and, indeed, realistic when one considers how a diary is written and the needs of the story: the reader has to be made aware of the background to Ann's situation, but the author does not allow her to reveal everything at once, as this would be clumsy and unnatural. Instead, Ann gradually fills us in on what has happened, with a little piece of information every so often. The **exposition** (see Literary Terms), starting with the most important incident, is subtle and natural. It also maintains interest by keeping the reader guessing (e.g. it is not until the end of Chapter 2 that we find out for certain that the narrator is a girl).

The fact that Ann's first action in response to the approach of the stranger is to go to the church and pray all morning tells us something about her spiritual nature. We also begin to admire her courage and her resilience as we realise what she has lived through. An atmosphere of suspense develops as we wonder with Ann who the stranger or strangers will be, and what they are like.

GLOSSARY   **dogwood** a wild shrub with dark red branches, greenish-white flowers and purple berries, found in woods and hedgerow
Amish a strict Mennonite sect, a Protestant group that originated in Switzerland, and settled in Pennsylvania in the east of the United States. Named after their leader, Jakob Amman, they are farmers who try to live and work simply, using horses instead of tractors and cars and avoiding the use of electricity
panel truck a small delivery van

CHAPTER *2*

May 23rd

Notice how careful Ann is.

Ann has reluctantly taken steps to cover up evidence of her existence, letting out the animals and digging up the vegetable garden. We learn that she has been lucky with the animals, except that one day David's dog Faro ran off. From the cave, where she has now moved for safety, she can see most of the valley; but she is sure the stranger will not see the cave as it is well hidden by trees.

Ann tells us how difficult it is to keep track of time, and how she would like to know when it is June 15th, her sixteenth birthday. She looks back on how she has survived, how lucky it was that the store was there in the valley, and how lucky it was that the war – which only lasted a week – had taken place in the spring, so she has the summer to get used to things and prepare for the winter.

Ann sees the smoke again, and calculates from its position that the stranger is on his way towards the valley. She decides that tomorrow she will go near the

A STRANGER ARRIVES

Is Ann right to take a gun?

top of Burden Hill and climb a tree to watch, taking one of her guns with her.

Ann writes about her water supply. There is a drilled well near the house, but this is now useless because it worked with an electric pump; similarly, she cannot use the electric water heater or the shower, so she has to carry water from one of two streams. She relates how, just in time, she realised that the larger of the two streams, Burden Creek, was poisoned, since it flows from outside the valley – just before using it she noticed dead fish and a dead turtle. The other, smaller, stream rises from a spring up the hill and flows into a large pond which contains pure water and live fish, which have been an important source of food.

Why is Ann now concerned about her appearance?

Ann has also begun to worry about her appearance. She is wearing men's blue jeans from the store, a man's work shirt, and boys' tennis shoes. Her hair is cut off square around her neck. She wonders about wearing a dress, but decides to wear the one pair of real slacks she has left.

May 24th

Ann has climbed a tree and seen that the stranger is a single man who is dressed in an orange, plastic-looking suit which covers him entirely, with a glass mask for his eyes. He has an air-tank on his back and he is pulling a wagon behind him, covered in the same orange material. Ann has to decide what to do.

COMMENT   In this chapter the reader is impressed by the way she has survived alone, and by the cautious but common-sense way in which she prepares for the stranger's arrival. Ann's caution in taking the rifle with her is sensible, and brings into the novel an important **motif** (see Literary Terms). Guns are to play an important part in the story. They can be important to survival, and it is notable that Ann, although a good shot, does not like guns. We learn that she has practised on tins and bottles rather than living creatures, but in taking the gun with her we see how common sense overrules her sensitivity. The fact that she does not expect to use it is **ironic** (see Literary Terms) and is one of many examples of her innate goodness and optimism.

The stranger's arrival in the valley brings an end to Ann's 'comfortable' existence. She has to destroy the garden she has worked so hard to create, and feels the need to leave her family home and live in a cave. This creates a sense of foreboding: 'I feel as if it is the beginning of the end' (p. 18).

The theme of survival is apparent in the story of the two streams: water is essential for life, but one of the streams has been polluted by the outside world and brings about death. Things – and people? – from the outside bring danger to the valley.

Ann's awareness of her appearance – she feels the need to dress like a girl – and the fact that this is a man approaching raises the question of sexuality, which will become important later.

GLOSSARY   **Guernseys** a breed of dairy cattle
a cord of wood a measure of cut wood, 128 cubic feet
bucksaw a large, heavy saw

A STRANGER ARRIVES

CHAPTER 3

Still May 24th

It is night and the stranger has entered Ann's house, or perhaps camped outside it in a small tent, for Ann cannot see too clearly. Ann tells of the man's reaction when he saw the green of the valley and the living trees. Anxious to take off his mask, he used two Geiger counters to check for radiation. Then he removed his mask and cheered – the first voice Ann had heard for a very long time, except for her own when she had sung sometimes. Ann liked the sound of his voice and her first reaction had been to run down and reveal herself, but she resisted. Ann had noticed he looked thin and not very healthy, but also 'rather poetic' (p. 27).

Having taken a gun out of his wagon, he had walked around the house, looked in every window and called again before entering. Ann feared she had left some evidence of her presence behind. After coming back out of the house twenty minutes later, he had set up his tent, made a fire and cooked a meal.

Ann believes he is now asleep and works out that the orange plastic material of the suit, the tent and the wagon cover is for keeping out radiation. She is still afraid but also feels it is '*companionable* to know there is someone else in the valley' (p. 30).

May 25th

Ann fears the stranger has made a mistake, and recounts the lead-up to it. When she came out of the cave he was already awake. Having taken from his wagon a larger gun, he shot one of Ann's chickens. This shocks her, since this is not the accepted way to kill a chicken. Coming across the pond, he had seen the minnows. He checked the water with his Geiger counter, then drank some, realising it was pure. After fetching some provisions from the store, he suddenly fired into some bushes, presumably at a rabbit. He missed.

Could Ann have prevented the stranger's mistake? He then made his mistake. He went swimming and had a bath, but in the wrong stream, the contaminated Burden Creek. He had removed his clothing and carelessly jumped in, not noticing the dead grass and weeds on the banks or the absence of fish. Ann does not know for certain what is wrong with the water, and therefore how bad a mistake he has made. She hopes it hasn't killed him.

COMMENT   The fact that Ann likes the sound of the man's voice, and comments on his wild and poetic appearance suggest the beginnings of an attraction to the stranger.

The stranger's use of the gun to kill the chicken and his reckless shot at the rabbit reveal a violence and a lack of restraint which contrast starkly with Ann's sensitivity.

Ann's thoughtful and common-sense approach to survival is highlighted by his careless leap into the poisoned water.

Ann still decides to wait and watch, despite her concern for his well-being.

GLOSSARY   **Geiger counter** an instrument used to measure radioactivity levels, named after Hans Geiger, a German physicist
carbine a light automatic rifle
bolt-action a rifle where the breechblock takes the form of a manually operated sliding rod
pump a rifle where a backward and forward movement of a lever ejects the empty case, cocks the rifle, and loads a new round
fescue a type of grass

CHAPTER 4

Still May 25th

Ann is in the cave at night. Strangely, Faro has returned. He is very thin and has lost half the hair from his left side. Faro is a mongrel who enjoyed hunting; hearing the gunshots probably brought him back. The man tries to befriend the dog by feeding it chicken, but then Faro picks up Ann's trail and runs towards the

A STRANGER ARRIVES

cave. Fortunately for Ann, the man is unable to follow the dog, but Ann realises that Faro may soon betray her presence. Ann then starts considering why that should be such a bad thing. Being alone for nearly a year; she had longed for someone to arrive, but now she considers the possibility that this may not be a good man. She continues to wait and watch to find out what he is like.

May 26th

According to her calendar, Ann believes it to be Sunday. Normally she would go to church and make it a day of rest. The man cooks breakfast quickly, and feeds Faro, who is still wary of him. The man goes into the store and comes out with new clothes on, making him look younger, 'thirty or thirty-two'. Walking towards the far end of the valley, the man finds the point where Burden Creek and the smaller stream join. Here, the difference between the smaller stream, full of fresh water life, and the dead Burden Creek is clear, though Ann is not sure if the man notices.

The stranger explores Ann's valley.

Ann tells us something of the geography of the valley and the fact that it was said to have its own weather due to its enclosed nature.

On his way back to the house, the man stops, sits down and is very sick. He collapses a further three times before reaching his tent and crawling inside. Ann hopes he will be better in the morning.

COMMENT

Faro's arrival can be compared to that of the stranger: it is a sign of hope, but also a potential danger.

We have evidence of Ann's natural possessiveness over 'her' valley: in the last chapter she was mildly annoyed at the man's shooting of one of her chickens, his entry into her house, and his building a fire with her wood. Now she speaks of his using her plates ('mine!') and her clothes ('*My* clothes').

CHAPTER 5

May 27th

Faro seems to be taking to the stranger and this makes Ann worried. Meanwhile, Ann knows the man is ill but not how seriously. He has remained in his tent: has he decided just to rest, or is he very ill, or even dying?

This morning Ann dreamt it was her father in the tent, ill, and that her whole family were in the house again. She had become used to the idea of being alone, probably forever, but now with the arrival of the man, she cannot bear this thought. Even though he is a stranger and she is afraid of him, she worries about his being ill, so she decides to go down to the tent, warily, with a gun.

May 28th

Who is Edward?

Ann is back in the house, in her own room. She had gone down to the tent and discovered the man lying there in his own vomit. As she touched his hand, the man said, 'Edward … Edward?' and also mentioned the word 'bullets' in his delirium. Ann is worried because she does not have the knowledge to take care of him. She cleans the man up, and brings him some soup.

He improves slightly and the next morning says he needs to know what made him ill. Ann explains that it was his bath in Burden Creek, and he realises his mistake in not testing the water. Using the Geiger counter, Ann tests the area by the water where he bathed. When he hears the result he realises he has radiation poisoning, about which he knows a great deal. Although he seems better, he explains the sickness comes in stages, and that soon he will become much worse again. He will have no resistance to germs, so Ann decides that she must try to prevent his catching an infection; she will also try to get him into the house, where it is drier and warmer. She realises she still does not know his name.

COMMENT

Dreams are important in this novel. The lonely world Ann has inhabited would be a severe trial for anyone, and she has dealt with this strongly in her waking life. She has shown tremendous self-discipline, but she cannot control her dreams, where she feels joyful at the idea that her family are back; this reveals her submerged grief.

Ann's natural goodness and compassion overcome her fear and caution as she decides to find out how ill the man really is.

Ann's bravery and common sense are revealed again in her reaction to the man's illness and her decision to nurse him. Her practical nature helps her to cope.

The man's fevered reference to 'Edward' gives us a tantalising hint of something that is troubling him. The reader feels the urge to read on and find out what this means.

GLOSSARY　　**anaemia** deficiency of red blood cells
　　　　　　　pneumonia acute inflammation of the lungs
　　　　　　　dysentery an infection of the intestine

Identify the speaker.

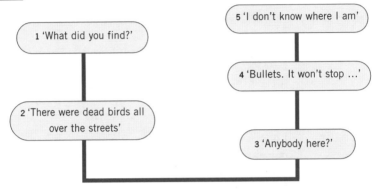

5 'I don't know where I am'

1 'What did you find?'

4 'Bullets. It won't stop ...'

2 'There were dead birds all over the streets'

3 'Anybody here?'

Identify the person(s) 'to whom' this comment refers.

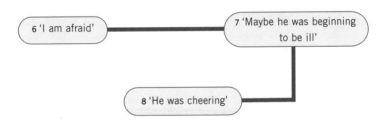

6 'I am afraid'

7 'Maybe he was beginning to be ill'

8 'He was cheering'

Check your answers on page 91.

B *Consider these issues.*

a What significance the diary format has in the telling of the story.

b What we know about Ann's life before the war and how it prepared her for solitude.

c What the reader has learnt about the man so far and what we feel we need to know.

d The way in which the man, like other things from outside the valley, presents a threat and a sense of danger.

e The **symbolism** (see Literary Terms) of guns, water, birds and radiation.

f Ann's mixed emotions over the arrival of the stranger.

CHAPTERS 6–10: NURSING THE SICK

CHAPTER 6

May 29th

Ann tells us that the man is called John R. Loomis, and that he seems much better. Loomis asks, somewhat suspiciously, if she is alone. Ann reveals she found out later he was a scientist, but his statements and questions suggest this. He tells his story and Ann tells hers. He says that he had seen no life until now on his ten week journey from Ithaca, in New York state.

Loomis has been sleeping in the tent because it is radiation-proof but now he realises the valley is safe and accepts Ann's offer to stay in the house. He goes on to tell Ann more of his background as an organic chemist working with the Nobel prizewinner, Professor Kylmer. In a secret laboratory built in the mountains they had discovered a way of making magnetic plastic, or 'polapoly' as they named it, which could stop, or at least deflect radiation. They developed a suit made of this substance, together with a portable device for filtering water and air. After three years of work they had

Consider the way in which the people in the Air Force fallout shelter died.

produced a single pilot model of each, and these were what Loomis had used on his journey – the suit and the wagon. But the war had broken out before these items could be mass-produced. When the bombing began, Loomis says he was alone in the laboratory, surviving because it was eighty feet underground and cut out of solid rock. He had waited three months to see if the outside radiation levels would drop, and then began to make excursions to the outside world, finding only death.

Why is Loomis so shocked when Ann mentions Edward?

Ann asks him about Edward. He seems shocked, but then tells her that Edward was a man who had worked in the laboratory with himself and Professor Kylmer. Loomis was unaware that he had mentioned his name.

COMMENT   Ann takes care to take a bath and improve her appearance. She is aware of Loomis as 'company'.

She is also aware of Loomis as a scientist: 'scientists won't just accept things – they always have to try to figure them out' (p. 62). This becomes important later.

Robert O'Brien allows Loomis to give scientific reasons why he has been able to survive, and the same is done for the valley: this increases the reader's belief in the narrative.

Loomis's reaction to Ann's knowledge of Edward creates more suspense at the end of the chapter.

GLOSSARY   **Cornell** a famous American university

Nobel prize a prestigious award given annually for work done in the fields of chemistry, physics, medicine, literature, and peace

the Pentagon the headquarters of the United States Defence Department in Arlington, Virginia, named after the building's shape

asphyxiation suffocation

CHAPTER 7

June 3rd

Ann has been keeping track of Loomis's temperature. She has suggested she give him some aspirin but he thinks they should save it. Ann has decided to 'cook better meals' now she has this companion to look after – she had often not bothered when she was by herself. She decides to dig over the garden again and plant some seeds, in the hope it is not too late, but realises she needs more space because there are now two mouths to feed. This proves difficult, and as she is toiling Loomis suggests she uses the tractor. Ann comments that she has no petrol – there are two pumps at the store but they work with electricity. Loomis tells her he could take off the electric motors and make them work by hand.

NURSING THE SICK

They watch the sun setting before returning to the house, Loomis walking unaided. He sits in her father's chair by the fireplace. Ann asks if Loomis would like a book. He does not, but when she suggests that she play the piano he is more enthusiastic. She plays from her study books and from a hymn book. Loomis is complimentary and tells Ann, 'This is the best evening I have ever spent'. When Ann replies, 'Ever? You mean since the war' Loomis becomes angry: 'I said "ever"' (p. 81). She puts this reaction down to the fever, and he goes to bed.

Playing the hymns has made Ann feel sad. She remembers going to Sunday School with her family, and a picture book she had called *The Bible Letter Book*. The first page was 'A is for Adam', and the last page was 'Z is for Zachariah'. Since Adam was the first man, she had assumed for a long time that Zachariah must be the last man.

Zachariah is a minor Jewish Prophet in the Old Testament.

Ann wishes she were back in the cave again. She is about to go, when she hears Loomis talking loudly in his sleep. He is talking to Edward. He says that Mary and Billy are dead. Then, 'Get away. I warn you. Get away from –' (p. 84) followed by a groan, and silence. Ann decides not to go to the cave, since Loomis might need help.

COMMENT   The chapter contrasts Ann's artistic tendencies with Loomis's scientific frame of mind. Loomis's scientific background looks like it will prove useful, and indicates that, however practical Ann may be, her lack of technical knowledge would have been a disadvantage to her.

There are indications that Loomis and Ann could have a partnership and, indeed, a relationship, which could be mutually beneficial.

The religious side to Ann's character is emphasised again. Through the novel's title we are led to consider the differences between Ann and Loomis's situation – the last man and woman on earth? – and that of Adam and Eve – the first man and woman.

The harmony of the piano-playing scene is ruined by Loomis's angry outburst. If it was his best evening ever, what does that say about his existence up until now?

Loomis's nightmare creates more tension and suspicion.

GLOSSARY   **'Für Elise'** a piece for piano by Beethoven (1770–1827), a German composer

CHAPTER 8

June 3rd (continued)

Ann has had a dream, remembering her mother walking across a field in early June gathering cress and poke greens. Together with dandelion leaves these would make a salad, and Ann takes a basket to collect these items. Having collected the plants, Ann notices a crabapple tree in full bloom. The flowers make her mind drift to weddings and she decides that if she ever got married, it would have to be in May, or early June, with apple blossom in the church. She remembers her first real date, with a boy from junior high school. Then

Does Ann really think marriage to Loomis is likely?

her thoughts turn to the possibility of marriage to Loomis. She thinks about having children some day, but then she is overcome with a feeling of sadness for

NURSING THE SICK

her mother and puts the thoughts out of her head. She cuts a branch of the apple blossom as a bouquet for Loomis's sickroom.

Loomis has gone to Burden Creek to test the water and has realised that Ann's results were correct – he has indeed taken a large dose of radiation. His thoughts turn to using the poisoned stream to create electricity by building a dam that could run a small generator. He could do this if he had an electric motor, and Ann remembers there are two or three in the barn. The electricity could power a light, a refrigerator and perhaps a freezer.

What could Loomis's enthusiasm for going fishing tell us about his background?

After breakfast, Ann says she is going fishing. Loomis has never fished before and wants to come with her. On the way to the pond, however, he collapses. He has anaemia and he is helped back to the house. After fishing alone, Ann dismantles the old wood-coal stove from the barn and pulls it out, but she will need help to get it on the cart and bring it to the house. She gets out the best china and they eat. Then Ann finds a set of books called *The Farm Mechanic* which Loomis reads.

COMMENT

Dreams play an important part in *Z for Zachariah*. Here, as later, a dream helps Ann. Loomis's dreams, by contrast, are nightmares which create cause for concern. Ann's optimistic nature is apparent as she looks forward to the possibility of marrying Loomis and bearing children.

Ann's naïvety and sense of what is traditional and appropriate come over in her decision that the wedding will have to be in church, with words from the *Book of Prayer*.

This chapter has an optimistic tone. Notice the **symbolism** (see Literary Terms) of the apple blossom and how it is used later in the novel (see Comment on p. 35 of these Notes).

GLOSSARY   **poke greens** edible wild plants
junior high school similar to a British middle school, students moving on at about fourteen years of age
masonite a type of dark brown hardboard
Thanksgiving an annual holiday, in thanksgiving to God, held on the fourth Thursday in November in the USA

CHAPTER 9

June 3rd (continued)

Contrast Ann's excitement about starting the tractor to Loomis's lack of emotion.

Ann gets the tractor running, having been told by Loomis how to get the petrol pumps operating. Ann plans her planting, showing her knowledge of farming. As she drives the tractor she feels like singing, and she recites a poem to herself. It is brought to mind by thoughts of her responsibility to the planet. As Ann ploughs she notices eleven crows in the sky, attracted by the noise of the tractor.

That night Loomis's temperature rises considerably.

COMMENT

Optimism again radiates throughout this chapter: notice how the sun comes out when Ann is ploughing, and the appearance of the crows, once classed as pests, but now **symbols** (see Literary Terms) of life and hope. Ann's love of singing and poetry again throws light on her optimistic nature. She has put out of her mind up to now the fact that the supplies in the store will not last forever. Contrast this with Loomis's practicality in saving the V-belt for future use.

GLOSSARY   **squash** a marrow-like vegetable
hominy coarsely ground corn boiled with milk or water

CHAPTER 10

June 3rd (Continued)

The fever has made Loomis afraid to be left alone. Ann wishes she were a trained nurse, and wishes she had warned Loomis about the water he bathed in. She does not tell him about her wishes with relation to marriage. When Ann goes to milk the cow Loomis sits up in bed and calls for her; he has imagined things in his feverish state but he will not tell her what.

Consider Ann's
reaction when
Loomis points the
gun at her.

She has to go to the brook for more water, and to the store for provisions. When she returns, Loomis staggers from the house and grabs the carbine rifle from his wagon. He shoots at the second floor of the house, then aims the gun at Ann. She remains calm and talks to him; he claims he had thought he had heard someone in the house. Ann takes the gun from his hands and returns it to the wagon. She puts Loomis back to bed and inspects the damage, which is minimal.

Still fevered, Loomis mentions Edward, and asks if he has gone. Ann tells him he has been dreaming again. He realises this and says that Edward is dead. Ann wonders why he wanted to kill his friend.

COMMENT

Notice how Loomis calls Ann by both forename and surname, 'Ann Burden', while Ann calls him 'Mr Loomis'. They still hardly know one another.

'Poor Ann Burden … You're going to wish I had never come' (p. 110) – here, Loomis is referring to his illness, but his words are packed with **irony** (see Literary Terms) in the light of what happens later.

Ann demonstrates her sensitivity and caring nature in looking after Loomis, and in her courage when he confronts her with the gun. Notice that this incident is mirrored at the end of the novel.

There is more destruction brought to the valley by Loomis, and the suspense grows when we learn that Edward is dead.

GLOSSARY   **steeped** soaked

EST YOURSELF (Chapters 6–10)

 Identify the speaker.

1 'Amazing'

2 'Get away. I warn you'

4 'It's started'

3 'Good Faro'

Identify the person(s) 'to whom' this comment refers.

5 'It turns out he is a real expert on the subject'

6 'I suppose they kept going too long'

Check your answers on page 91.

B *Consider these issues.*

a How well Ann copes with Loomis's illness.

b The differences shown in these chapters between Ann and Loomis.

c What Loomis's background may have been like, as a child and as a young man.

d Loomis as a danger to Ann and life in the valley.

e Ann's romantic, religious and artistic nature.

f The significance of the novel's title.

g The author's use of the **symbolism** (see Literary Terms) of nature.

CHAPTERS 11–15: LIVING WITH A MURDERER

CHAPTER 11

June 4th

Loomis's temperature has reached one hundred and six, the highest reading the thermometer can show. Ann tries her best to reduce this by rubbing him with alcohol. Loomis's nightmares continue, dreaming that Edward is there, in the room and threatening him. Ann is beginning to piece together the story, realising that Loomis and Edward 'were not friends at all, but enemies, at least at the end' (p. 121). When Ann brings Loomis breakfast he drifts in and out of his hallucination. He tries to get out of bed and Ann holds him down, with Loomis whispering, 'He'll steal the suit' (p. 122). Ann tells him the suit is in the wagon, but this incites Loomis to try to get out of bed again. Loomis is weak, and Ann can easily hold him down, but she is worried that if he falls he will injure himself and she will not be able to put him into bed again. So Ann decides to stay in the room with him, and when he is asleep, go out to feed Faro and bring in the suit. Ann is affected by Loomis's dreams, and half expects to see Edward herself.

Ann is only concerned with Loomis's well-being.

Afternoon

Ann manages to piece together the story of Edward and Loomis. The two scientists were together in the underground laboratory when the bombing began. Edward wanted to go and look for his wife, Mary, and son, Billy. In the laboratory was the one suit in the world which would allow him to venture out into the radioactive, polluted air. Loomis would not allow Edward to use the suit: everyone outside was dead, he argued; and what would happen if Edward did not return with the suit? Loomis had a gun. He swore at Edward and threatened him as Edward tried to leave with the suit.

Loomis collapses again on his bed, leaving Ann to wonder if he had really shot Edward. As Loomis sleeps again, Ann inspects the suit and her worst fears are confirmed: there are three patched bullet holes across the middle of the chest, and Ann knows that if Edward had been wearing the suit when they were fired he would certainly have been killed.

Night Loomis sleeps peacefully, but Ann realises there is nothing more she can do for him. She takes a Bible and walks to the church to pray for him.

COMMENT Notice the **hookline** (see Literary Terms) at the beginning of the chapter: 'This is a terrible day' (p. 120) creates more suspense and pulls the reader into the story once more.

Ann can see both sides of the argument between Loomis and Edward. She is very fair and can see how it would be pointless to search for a wife and child who are almost certainly dead. But she also identifies with Edward: 'Poor Edward … I know how he felt' (p. 125).

'One suit, and two people' – compare this with the situation now, with Ann and Loomis together in the valley.

We now suspect that Loomis is a murderer, capable of killing to gain what he wants; but despite what Ann has heard, she does not give up caring for him.

CHAPTER 12

June 5th   Loomis has lived through the night, although at one point Ann was sure he had died. The strain is beginning to tell on her; she feels dizzy and ill, and goes to the church again. This time, she knows it is for her own benefit. She is fatalistic, realising that her presence will now make no difference to whether Loomis lives or dies. She is also worried about what she heard from Loomis about the events in the laboratory.

In the church Faro discovers a baby crow which had fallen from a nest built up in the roof. Ann picks it up and places it in the grass outside, and the crows fly down to it. She admits to being a little superstitious, and thinks of this as a good omen.

Evening   Loomis's condition is unchanged. Ann decides to read to him, thinking first of the Bible, but then deciding on Gray's 'Elegy Written in a Country Churchyard'. She also considers playing the piano, as much for her benefit as his.

Ann again considers the rights and wrongs of Loomis's actions in the laboratory. In a way, she believes what he did was in self-defence: if Edward had gone, Loomis would have eventually run out of food, water or air and he would have died. Loomis might also have been thinking about saving the suit for humanity. But what if Edward was sensible or honest? What if Loomis wanted the suit for himself? She does not know enough about either Edward or Loomis.

June 6th   Ann goes to church again and prays. Loomis has now lain motionless for more than thirty-two hours, but

Ann does not want to give up. The baby bird has gone, and Ann is sure it has been returned to its nest. On the way back to the house she picks wild roses and puts them in a vase in Loomis's room. The apple blossoms have wilted and fallen off. Loomis's respiration has decreased, although Ann does not know if this is a good thing or a bad thing. She plays the piano.

COMMENT   We can easily imagine the strain on Ann, with Loomis near death, and on top of that, the knowledge that this man, perhaps the only man left alive on earth, is probably a murderer.

Ann acknowledges the **symbolism** (see Literary Terms) of the bird, a sign of life and hope. She tells us that she once thought of birds as prayers, flying up to heaven.

Ann speaks of doing things for her own benefit: she feels comfort in prayer, poetry, and music.

The apple blossom, once the **symbol** (see Literary Terms) of her projected happy future with Loomis, has died; this future has now seemingly been put in jeopardy.

GLOSSARY   **cupola** a roof in the form of a dome
two-by-four planks of wood, two inches thick, four inches wide
'Elegy Written in a Country Churchyard' a famous poem written by
Thomas Gray (1716–71) in 1750

CHAPTER 13

June 7th   Loomis is better. Ann changes his bed linen and pyjamas. It is a messy job and Ann realises she was not cut out to be a nurse. She had once considered it, but she had decided she wanted to be a teacher instead. She reflects that these and other plans are effectively over. One of her plans had been to buy books; we learn that she loves books. She wonders if Loomis could go to the library and bookstore in Ogdentown and bring back books. Would he be interested, seeing as he does not appear to be much of a reader? Would the books be safe or contaminated? Could Ann go herself, in the suit? These thoughts are suddenly clouded by thoughts of Edward.

June 8th   Loomis awakes. His temperature is down, but he is extremely thin. Ann thinks about food for him and wishes she had the stove. Using the tractor, she brings it to the house and, with a little difficulty, rebuilds it. She only needs some stovepipe and an elbow to connect it to the kitchen chimney. She is elated – having the stove there is 'like getting a Christmas present' (p. 146).

COMMENT   We see that Ann's plans for a career have always been influenced by her desire to help people.

Ann despairs for a moment, because her ambitions cannot be fulfilled, but the rest of the chapter has an atmosphere of hope and optimism. Loomis is recovering; she maintains a sense of purpose, to survive and improve the quality of their existence, by rebuilding the stove.

Books will also improve the quality of Ann's life, but there is still the shadow of Loomis's attitude to her plans, and the fear of his jealous possessiveness over the suit. Her desire is similar to Edward's desire – and Loomis killed Edward.

CHAPTER 14

June 15th   It is Ann's birthday. She is sixteen, and, with the stove now fully connected, she has roasted a chicken and baked a cake, which, despite her inexperience, has turned out perfectly. They are also celebrating Loomis's recovery, although he still cannot walk.

Ann starts to turn her thoughts to the future again: the garden needs attention and she needs to plant seeds.

Ann had intended to keep these problems to herself, but Loomis had enquired about the tractor and the planting. His tone was nervous and suspicious. Ann admits that the corn is not yet planted, that she had not dared tell Loomis when he was so ill. When she tells Loomis that she had gone to church – three times – he is angry and abrupt. She calms him by telling him that her family had planted corn before at this time, and even later, and it had fared well. But she is startled by his tone and attitude – Ann had always thought of the valley as her own, but now she realises Loomis would be living there too.

Why is Loomis so angry that Ann went to church?

Ann harrows the soil, and plants most of the corn. She starts to cook but then hears Loomis fall; he has tried to get out of bed. He refuses help and tells Ann not to watch as he awkwardly returns to bed. He asks for drawing instruments and paper.

COMMENT   Ann's diary entries are no longer written on a day-to-day basis. This indicates the pressure she is under and how busy she is. The story is again recounted by telling the reader the important facts, building up suspense, and following them by **flashbacks** (see Literary Terms) to the details of the events.

The chapter seems optimistic enough, but Loomis again taints the atmosphere with his aggressive insistence not to be helped and his reaction to her delay with the planting.

As it becomes obvious that Loomis will recover, it also becomes obvious that he sees the valley as his as well as Ann's. Ann's reaction to this reveals her sense of fairness and tolerance.

Ann's reference to this as 'one of the best of weeks' (p. 147) is perhaps **ironic** (see Literary Terms) in the light of Loomis's behaviour.

CHAPTER 15

June 22nd

Another week has passed and Loomis has gradually learned to walk again. He does this in private, but Ann is pleased at his progress.

Loomis is designing the water-powered generator, and finds the magazines inadequate. When he says he needs books, Ann brings up the idea of going to the library in Ogdentown. Ann touches on her desire to read works of literature but Loomis is not interested. When he dismisses the idea because he is unable to walk that far, Ann makes the mistake of saying that she could go, if he lent her the suit. His anger at this suggestion is apparent. Loomis then gives a logical reason for Ann's not going: it would be foolish to risk its loss for the sake of a few novels, and if something happened to Ann and she did not return, he would be stranded. Ann sees the sense of the argument, but still retains some hope.

Is Ann's suggestion totally unreasonable, as Loomis suggests?

Ann suggests putting a chair for Loomis on the front porch. He would like it on the back porch, where he can see her doing the planting. Ann says the corn is rising, but Loomis is not satisfied: he asks why she had not planted beets and wheat, for sugar and flour. Ann had thought about these, but before the tractor was working, and there was only so much she could do. Loomis calls her 'foolish and short-sighted' (p. 164) and talks about the valley as being the whole world, where they should be thinking about starting a colony which will last permanently. Ann had had these thoughts, but now she feels uneasy.

COMMENT   As Loomis becomes stronger, he becomes increasingly domineering, and Ann is beginning to feel threatened. He is making decisions and beginning to take control; Ann is conceding that he is right and good-naturedly allowing him to do this.

The contrast between Ann and Loomis is never more evident than in his attitude to books. For him the only worthwhile books are 'practical' ones. Ann's quality of life would be much improved by literature and the world of the imagination.

Loomis is patronising towards Ann. In calling her 'foolish and short-sighted' (p. 164) he is being unfair and short-sighted himself when one considers what Ann has done for him, and what she has achieved on her own.

Loomis is also disparaging about Ann's religious instincts – notice how he refers to 'your church'.

Loomis talks about starting a colony. This obviously has implications: to survive on a long-term basis, Loomis and Ann must produce offspring, just as the cattle must also be used for breeding.

Power and control are centred on the suit. When he tells Ann she must never touch it, Loomis's words are echoes of what she heard him say to Edward in Chapter 11.

A *Identify the speaker.*

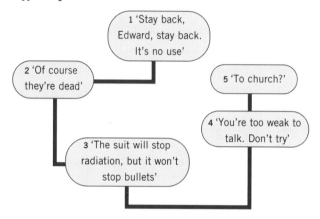

1 'Stay back, Edward, stay back. It's no use'

2 'Of course they're dead'

5 'To church?'

4 'You're too weak to talk. Don't try'

3 'The suit will stop radiation, but it won't stop bullets'

Identify the person(s) 'to whom' this comment refers.

6 'you're a thief and a liar'

7 'He may have been thinking not just of himself, but of human survival'

Check your answers on page 91.

B *Consider these issues.*

a Ann's fair-mindedness when confronted by the reality of what Loomis has done.

b The **symbolism** (see Literary Terms) of the bird which has fallen from the nest.

c The difference between Ann's attitude to books and that of Loomis.

d Loomis's scientific disposition compared with Ann's artistic, spiritual nature.

e How optimism is often built up, only to be clouded by subsequent events.

f Loomis's gradual improvement in health, accompanied by his gradual desire to become the dominant partner in the relationship.

CHAPTERS 16–20: ATTACKED AND HUNTED

CHAPTER 16

June 24th

Ann is growing more and more uneasy. She has planted wheat and beets, following Loomis's outburst. As she suggested, she has put a chair on the front porch, and one on the back porch. Despite the fact that the back porch is the less comfortable place to be, this is where Loomis insists he will sit. He watches while Ann works.

Ann later joins him on the front porch. She has realised that she knows nothing about him, does not understand him. She has worked out a theory that he has tried to blot out the past – the murder of Edward, the long walk through the dead countryside – because it was so horrible. She is sensible enough not to try to discuss Edward, but she tries to start up a conversation, hoping to gain a little more information about the times before that. She finds out that he is from a poor background in Nyack, New York, and that he was in the Navy for four years. Ann then asks him if he ever got married. At this, Loomis grabs Ann's hand and pulls her towards him. He says, 'No, I never got married. Why did you ask that?' (p. 171) and holds Ann's hand in both of his.

Is Ann any the wiser about Loomis's background?

Ann is startled, and then feels 'embarrassed, and awkward, and afraid' (p. 171) – embarrassed, strangely, because his hands are softer than hers; awkward because he has pulled her off balance on his chair; and afraid because when she tries to pull away he tightens his grip. He shows no gentleness and has no expression on his face. He will not relax his grip until she answers his question, but when he tightens his grip even more and pulls Ann even further off balance she falls forward and accidentally hits him in the face. She releases herself but Loomis tells her she should not have done so. Ann

ATTACKED AND HUNTED

apologises and retires to the kitchen, as Loomis says, 'You held my hand once before' (p. 173).

In the kitchen Ann is shaking and she feels about to cry but stops herself. She tries to calm down, telling herself it was just a 'pass': it had happened to girls at school on dates. However, it is very different when there is nobody around – in Ann's case, perhaps nobody in the world! To comfort herself, Ann imagines that her family are coming back. She calms herself and continues with dinner.

Loomis returns to the bedroom and when Ann brings his food he acts as if nothing had happened, but they do not talk. Ann remembers when she did hold his hand: for several hours on the night he was most ill, but she realises this is not the same thing. She realises Loomis is taking charge, taking possession, and she feels uneasy.

COMMENT   Loomis is gradually taking control. Ann describes him as 'rather like an overseer' (p. 167), and he is now stronger than Ann. There are **ironic** (see Literary Terms) reversals of situation in this chapter. Ann once watched over Loomis, when he was ill; now he watches over her as if to check on her work. She once held his hand gently, nursing him; now he holds her hand aggressively, as if possessing her.

Ann tries to justify Loomis's secrecy when talking about his past, just as she has tried to see both sides of the story before.

We do not know for sure what Loomis's intentions are, because we see everything through Ann's eyes. Perhaps he does believe that Ann's reference to marriage indicates that she is sexually attracted to him, but we know of Loomis's cold attitude towards founding a colony.

Ann has shown great strength of character to keep her family from her conscious thoughts. Now she needs to think of them to deal with this situation.

GLOSSARY   **overseer** the person on a plantation who watched over the slaves to ensure they did their work

naval ordnance laboratory a laboratory where work on military equipment is carried out for the Navy

chemistry major a student whose main subject at university is chemistry

CHAPTER 17

June 30th

Note the use of flashback (see Literary Terms) once Ann has told us she is back in the cave.

Ann has returned to the cave, and recounts the events which have led to this drastic action. On the night of the 'pass' Ann could not sleep; the next day she felt 'everything had changed' but she tried to get on with her chores.

Although Ann is feeling strained and tense, Loomis acts as though nothing has happened. He watches her work again, making Ann feel under more pressure. At dinner, Loomis decides he will not eat in bed any more, but at the table. He tries to make conversation, and attempts to pay her compliments about the corn and the vegetable garden.

Loomis asks Ann to read to him again. She does so against her will, although she realises he is not even listening. She begins to feel nervous and afraid. She even feels he is trying to play some kind of trick on her. But she puts this thought from her mind and again tries to justify his behaviour.

COMMENT   Ann tells us how she feels better working in the open air. Her love of natural things contrasts with Loomis's unnatural behaviour.

ATTACKED AND HUNTED

Loomis uses Ann's love of reading to gain more power over her. She does not want to read, but feels compelled.

Ann tries to make herself believe that Loomis's request is reasonable enough, but her sensitivity makes her realise that there is something threatening in this.

Ann reads Gray's 'Elegy Written in a Country Churchyard' again, and also Jane Austen's *Pride and Prejudice*, in which two people at first dislike one another but later fall in love and marry – this could perhaps be seen as a reversal of what has happened in *Z for Zachariah*.

CHAPTER 18

*Still June
30th*

*Loomis is spoiling
everything that
Ann used to enjoy.*

Ann describes the next night, which was even worse. This time he has asked her to play the piano. As she plays, with her back to Loomis, she is wary of him. She worries he will creep up behind her. He taps his cane and she turns around, startled. He claims his can had slipped but she does not believe him, and she is trembling so much she has to stop. She thinks he is deliberately trying to unnerve her.

The next evening he does not ask her to read or play the piano, so she goes for a walk with Faro. At the church she hears the two crows and their young ones in the belfry. On her way back, she sees Loomis walking, unaided, to the wagon. He appears to be checking the safe-suit. After a short time, Ann returns to the house, goes to her bedroom, and, feeling uneasy, sits on the bed, having decided not to undress.

She falls asleep but awakes in the darkness to hear Faro growl and run out of the room. Then she realises why: Loomis is in the room with her. He thinks she is asleep, and he creeps forward until he is next to her. He begins to touch her. Breathing quickly and loudly, he tries to pin her to the bed. She tries to escape, and after a prolonged scuffle, she hits back with her elbow and catches him in the throat, enabling her to run out of the door.

COMMENT

Loomis uses subtle ways to put pressure on Ann. He asks her to do things which she normally enjoys, such as playing the piano. But he taunts her – the tapping of his stick is almost certainly not accidental, and he knows he has her worried.

When Ann makes the excuse that she is tired, Loomis replies, 'Tired so soon?' (p. 184) He is being sarcastic and sexually threatening, just as he was when he held her hand.

The fact that Loomis walks to the wagon without the use of the cane suggests that he may have been pretending to be weaker than he actually is.

When Ann goes for her walk there is a return to the peace nature engenders in her. The crows are still there, and the young one she rescued is still thriving. But this can be seen as the calm before the storm, a lull before the violence of Loomis's attempt to rape her.

Loomis now tries to possess her fully. The writing is powerful and full of horrific action. We are reminded of Ann's fears in Chapter 1 about the arrival of a stranger: 'suppose it was someone mean, or even cruel, and brutal? A murderer?' (p. 10) Loomis has turned out to be all these things.

GLOSSARY

Clementi an Italian composer (1752–1832)

sonatina a short piece of music

andante piece of music to be played slowly

Heller a Hungarian composer (1815–1888)

ATTACKED AND HUNTED

whip-poor-wills birds native to North America, named after
their cry

fireflies flying insects which give off light from their tails

CHAPTER 19

June 30th
(continued)
Ann continues to recount the fateful night, and
tells us that she has never been so afraid. She runs
down the road, unsure of whether Loomis is
following her or not. She stops at the store and sits
there for an hour or more, watching the road. When
she has pulled her thoughts together she realises
she cannot return to the house. Remembering that
there are still blankets in the cave, Ann takes shirts
and shoes from the store by candlelight, and goes to
the cave.

The next morning, she observes the house, using the
binoculars which she had left in the cave several weeks
ago. Faro is the first to appear. The dog sniffs the
ground and begins to follow her trail. Luckily, Faro
goes towards the store, following the scent, and not
straight to the cave. Loomis cannot follow the dog's
movements from there, and Faro arrives at the cave ten
minutes later.

Ann makes a mistake: she should have fed Faro immediately, as she did every morning; she still has three tins of meat in the cave. But Faro returns to the house, looking for food, and Ann realises that the dog could betray her location to Loomis. Watching the house, Ann sees Loomis feed Faro, at the same time tying the dog to the porch rail with a long cord. Ann feels sorry for the dog as it unsuccessfully tries to escape.

Are Ann's hopes for a compromise realistic?

She starts thinking about her responsibilities, such as looking after the animals and the garden, and wonders whether she can work out a compromise. Could she still do the outdoor chores? Should she bring Loomis supplies from the store? She will not go into the house to cook, but she feels she cannot let Loomis starve, 'no matter what he had done'. Ann is willing to compromise, but she is unsure if Loomis will be, so she decides to go and talk to Loomis. She could do this from a distance. She sleeps, eats, and later on decides to build a fire in a way Loomis will not be able to see it.

COMMENT

The author effectively conveys to us Ann's fear with the details of her pounding heart and her dizziness. She jumps when the door of the store slams shut, and the cold wind and her shivering add to the atmosphere of fear, isolation and suspense. We identify with Ann and feel sympathy for her plight. Tension is further built up by the threat that Faro can be used to track her down.

The way Faro is tied up, and his reaction to this loss of freedom, causes Ann to sympathise with the dog, and she feels the need to release him. In many ways, it is also a parallel situation to the one in which Ann now finds herself.

Ann is still concerned about her 'duties' as she sees them. Her concern for Loomis, despite what he has

done to her, underlines her innate goodness, as does her
desire for compromise. She feels they can share the
valley – though this is perhaps somewhat naïve – and
she is sensible enough, and brave enough, to want to
talk things through.

CHAPTER 20

July 1st

Ann has realised that Loomis is definitely going to use
Faro to track her: he ties Faro on the electric cord leash,
but only for fifty yards or so before he limps back to the
house. Ann believes Loomis knows she is watching
him, and that he is playing some kind of game with
her. She assesses the resources she has in the cave: some
food, the two guns and ammunition and some other
essentials, but not a great deal. She realises she is
vulnerable if she sleeps in the cave, so she sleeps instead
on a small shelf, near where she has been building a
wall to conceal the fire.

The next morning, she goes to the house, by an indirect
route so Loomis will not know where she is coming
from. She stops on the road in front of the garden and
Loomis steps out onto the porch. Loomis tells her he
had thought and hoped she would come back. She is
stunned for a moment, but then realises she cannot
trust him again, and she tells him she is not coming
back. He asks why this is, and where she will stay. He
acts as if he has forgotten what he has done, but Ann
knows he is just pretending. She tells him that she is
willing to tend to the crops, the seeds, the garden and
the animals, as well as bring him water and food, if he
leaves her alone. He asks where she will go at night, but
Ann does not reveal where she is staying. Loomis
agrees to this, saying that he hopes Ann will change her
mind and 'act more like an adult and less like a
schoolgirl' (p. 204).

*Ann is not
convinced when
Loomis pretends
he has forgotten
what has
happened.*

After the conversation, Ann realises that Loomis is still plotting, that he has not really accepted her offer. She knows Faro must be tied up inside the house, in case she tried to release him and take him away. She has a vision of herself tied up like Faro, Loomis's prisoner. Ann puts the idea out of her mind and milks the cow, realising that its milk is drying up. She divides the milk fairly between herself and Loomis, and does the same with the eggs, vegetables, and groceries from the store. She is slightly optimistic that this system might work.

Notice how fairly Ann divides the food.

On her return to the cave, Ann completes work on her hidden fire, but then she sees Loomis, with Faro on the leash, tracking again. They get as far as the barn, where Loomis starts up the tractor and teaches himself how to drive it. Ann lights her fire and cooks dinner.

Why does Loomis teach himself to drive the tractor?

She wishes now that Loomis had never come to the valley; she does not wish him dead, just that he had perhaps found some other valley.

COMMENT

The threat that Loomis will use Faro to track Ann down now becomes frighteningly real. The only thing stopping him now is his lack of strength, but the knowledge that this will return heightens the tension.

Compare the 'game of chess' here with the reference to chess on pp. 254–5 of the novel.

Loomis is still playing games with Ann. She likens it to a game of chess, a game she does not want to be involved in: 'Only Mr Loomis wanted to be in it, and only he could win it' (p. 199).

Ann is again concerned with the basic necessities for living, and shows her humanity and concern by still trying to be absolutely fair to Loomis, sharing out the provisions and hoping he will accept her compromise.

Ann knows now, however, that Loomis is not sorry for what he has done. He has tried to rape her and he pretends nothing has happened. She realises that he wants to treat her as a possession, to keep her as much a prisoner as Faro. He tries again and again to find out where she is staying.

In Chapter 1, Ann thought that 'there are worse things than being alone' (p. 10). Now she realises this is true, but she still does not coarsen her humanity by wishing Loomis dead. She begins to wonder if there are similar valleys, with people still alive.

GLOSSARY   **burlap** a coarse fabric used for sacking

TEST YOURSELF (Chapters 16–20)

 Identify the speaker.

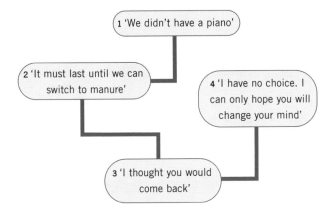

1 'We didn't have a piano'

2 'It must last until we can switch to manure'

4 'I have no choice. I can only hope you will change your mind'

3 'I thought you would come back'

Identify the person(s) 'to whom' this comment refers.

5 'there was nothing childlike about him'

6 'I will not change my mind'

Check your answers on page 91.

B *Consider these issues.*

a Ann's constant attempts to justify Loomis's behaviour and see some good in him.

b Ann's love of nature and that which is natural, in contrast to Loomis's unnatural actions.

c The way in which Loomis uses pastimes that Ann once enjoyed to threaten her.

d The power of the writing in the scenes leading up to, during, and just after the attempted rape.

e The similarities between Faro's position and Ann's.

CHAPTERS 21–26: LEAVING THE VALLEY

CHAPTER 21

August 4th
(I think)

We immediately learn that Ann has been shot by Loomis. She has not written for over a month because she was too ill and afraid. She has had to keep moving, and she is now hiding in thick woods high up in the south end of the valley. She shelters herself and her possessions in a hollow tree. She gives an account of the incidents which have occurred since July 1st.

For about ten days the compromise system seems to work. Ann does the chores and leaves food and provisions on the back porch for Loomis. Loomis, meanwhile, practises tracking with Faro, allowing the dog off the leash at times, and he also practises driving the tractor, on one occasion testing it to see how fast it can go.

On the morning of the tenth day (although Ann is not sure if this is accurate) Loomis changes his behaviour. He walks furtively towards the store, and then to the side of Burden Creek, where he hides in the trees and bushes. Ann realises that he is trying to find out where she is coming from, so she uses another route. She gathers eggs for Loomis. She realises she has forgotten to bring anything to carry eggs in for herself; she has also left behind her milk pail and her knife.

Ann makes a
mistake.

Ann takes Loomis's water can towards the pond, and then, out of sight, she runs back to the cave for the knife and the pail. She feels confident she has escaped detection but she is wrong. She completes some chores and goes to use the tractor to put fertiliser on the wheat, but finds out that the ignition key is missing. At first she thinks Loomis has dropped it, but then she realises he has taken it deliberately. She goes to ask him for it.

Loomis is ingratiatingly polite, and invites her in for lunch. She refuses, and ignores his question about where she will cook her half of the chicken. He says he has taken the key for safekeeping. When she tells him she needs it, he replies that he will have to think about it, threatening her that if she continues 'this stupidity' there are things they are going to have to go without. He suggests he might fertilise the wheat himself. Then he mentions the knife and pail, and goes in.

Loomis controls the tractor.

Ann realises the error she has made – he has obviously watched her going for the knife and pail, and has deduced that wherever she is staying is only a few minutes from the pond. Ann realises Loomis has taken the key because he fears she will steal the tractor, just as he had feared she would take the safe-suit and Faro.

COMMENT

The first two sentences of Chapter 21 are the most powerful **hooklines** (see Literary Terms) of the novel. They prepare the reader with a sense of suspense leading up to the conclusion of the novel.

Ann's lifestyle seems to have deteriorated to that of a hunted victim, while Loomis lives in the house that was once hers and her family's – the references to Burden Hill and Burden Creek emphasise this; she has been totally dispossessed. She is working for Loomis as he regains his strength – notice how he now moves with no apparent effort. This serves to underline the **irony** (see Literary Terms) of her situation.

Ann feels the loss of her Bible.

Ann stops off at the church once or twice, but 'It seemed strained' (p. 212). She still prays, and still has a sense of hope and faith in God, but the normality of her life has been irreparably altered.

Look at what has changed since Ann picked the apple blossom in Chapter 8.

Ann passes the crabapple tree on her way to the farm, recalling those earlier days when she had thoughts of having apple blossom at her wedding. The blossom has gone, to be replaced by bitter crabapples, **symbolic** (see Literary Terms) of how her life has since become bitter.

Ann still maintains a remarkable sense of honesty and fairness in her division of the food, but this is in contrast to Loomis's unscrupulousness, and it puts her in more danger as he grows stronger and healthier. Similarly, Ann has used the tractor for their mutual benefit, but Loomis now uses it for his own ends.

CHAPTER 22

August 4th (continued)

Ann knows that unlike when Loomis shot at the house, this time he is acting deliberately.

Ann has walked to the store after going fishing when she hears the tractor engine, so she runs up the hill to hide in the woods. She then watches in amazement as Loomis drives the tractor, steering with his left hand; in his right hand he carries a rifle. He stops the tractor near the store and, taking the ignition key, walks warily around before going in.

Ann sees Loomis's face appear at the window of the Kleins' living quarters on the first floor – he obviously believes Ann has been staying there. In fact, Ann has only been in the apartment once before, looking for books, She remembers feeling guilty about this intrusion, even though the Kleins were dead.

Ann sees Loomis come out of the store, go back in again, and then start doing something with the door. After he has finished and returned to the house, Ann walks down to the store to find that he has padlocked both the front and the back doors. She realises that now she will have to ask permission to use the tractor and to enter the store; or, worse still, he might not allow her to have the keys at all.

COMMENT

Ann wonders why he has the gun with him – Does he think she has a gun? Will he shoot her? The reader knows that at some point he will, since Ann

Ann sees that Loomis's actions are governed partly by fear.

has already told us so. The structure of the novel in relation to time becomes complex here. Ann is recounting past events, and in the middle of the chapter she goes further back in time to tell the reader of the time she ventured into the Kleins' apartment.

Ann's feeling of guilt at entering the Kleins' residence contrasts with Loomis's lack of concern. He has already taken over her home.

There is a certain **black humour** (see Literary Terms) in the picture of Loomis riding the tractor, rifle in hand 'like an Indian on horseback in an old Western movie, attacking a wagon train' (p. 225). The same filmic quality can be seen in Ann's observation that Loomis seems to be 'storming' the store.

CHAPTER 23

August 4th (continued)

Ann tells how she began the next day in a more optimistic frame of mind. She has recognised Loomis's obsession for being in charge, and she rationalises that his locking of the store is just a result of this. He wants to ration the provisions. However, she sees the other alternative: he could be trying to starve her into submission.

Is Ann right to try to talk to Loomis?

Ann begins to plan again. She realises that she cannot survive indefinitely on her provisions in the cave, and she bravely decides to walk to the house and to talk to him. As she stands in front of the house, she suddenly finds she has been shot in the ankle. A second shot misses, and Ann runs for her life. He stops shooting and she finds refuge in the trees. She examines the wound and finds it is not serious. She realises that she has no bandages or disinfectant, and washes the wound with soap at the cave.

Ann wonders about Loomis's shooting. She gradually comes to the frightening conclusion that he was not aiming to kill her, but to disable her – starvation would force her to return, and then he would keep her prisoner, using the gun as a threat. Hearing the tractor, Ann runs up the hill to the bushes. Loomis stops at the store. He has Faro with him, and, with the dog on the leash, he begins to track her. He has the small rifle, and he is obviously concerned that Ann might shoot at him.

Why doesn't Ann shoot Faro.

Ann runs to the cave, knowing she cannot stay there any more, and takes what she can carry, including the small rifle and a box of shells. Moving higher up the hill into the woods, Ann realises the danger Faro now poses, and decides she must shoot the dog. She watches and waits. Loomis stops, and she has Faro in her sights, but Faro perceives her presence. He gives a bark of greeting and Ann cannot go through with it.

Loomis and the dog arrive at the cave. Ann smells, then sees, smoke. She hears the tractor, and knows Loomis is returning to the house. Ann goes back to the cave to find her possessions burnt. Loomis has taken the tins of food and the other gun. She is devastated, but her main cause for concern is that she had decided to kill Faro – she feels this makes her as much a murderer as Loomis. She leaves the reader with the statement that in the end she did kill Faro, but 'not with the gun' (p. 241).

COMMENT Ann still tries to rationalise Loomis's behaviour. She at first cannot bring herself to believe that anyone could behave in such a callous manner. Her common sense takes over, however, but she still wants to talk and to compromise. Her innate sense of goodness and morality are shown throughout this chapter.

Robert O'Brien slowly works up towards the shooting incident, making it, when it comes, all the more shocking, especially when contrasted to Ann's generous intentions. Notice also how the author makes Ann recount the story in the present tense, making it more immediate and gripping.

Ann's despairing thought, 'why must he do it?' (p. 237) reveals her incomprehension of Loomis's behaviour.

Ann cannot bring herself to shoot Faro. Her sensitivity makes her believe that even the thought of killing the dog makes her a murderer like Loomis.

Ann has always shared the food and provisions. Now Loomis destroys everything he can, and takes the rest. **Symbolically** (see Literary Terms) he even destroys her last book. He has destroyed everything she holds dear.

The final paragraph of the chapter forces the reader to continue in order to discover why and how she eventually kills Faro. Note, though, that this technique is not entirely consistent with the diary since Faro does not die until August 6th.

GLOSSARY   **draw the bead** aim the rifle

CHAPTER 24

August 6th   Ann has been ill and feverish because of her wound but she is now feeling better. She feels more optimistic because she has made a plan: she has decided to steal the safe-suit and leave the valley. Loomis has not tried to track her again, although he could easily have done so. He perhaps did not know she was injured.

Is Ann's dream   Ann has had a dream about a class of schoolchildren
perhaps prophetic?   who cannot read and are waiting for a teacher. It has recurred night after night, and it has indicated to her that there is another place to live, where she is needed. She has come to the conclusion that Loomis is insane and that they cannot live in the same place. She will go

south, towards other valleys, and look for the children in her dream.

Ann has seen and heard Loomis working. Ann has survived by fishing and foraging, even sneaking down to steal vegetables from the garden. Life has been hungry and monotonous, and Ann, who has been taught from childhood that hatred is wrong, admits to herself that she would like to hurt Loomis. It is the memory of her burnt book which brings these thoughts most strongly to Ann's mind. Stealing the safe-suit would be her revenge.

Is this the first time Ann has contemplated taking the suit?

She puts off her plan of action until one day when she sees that Loomis has left the door to the store open. She needs supplies for the journey so she takes her chance. She is fifty yards from the road when a shot rings out. It misses her and she flees back up to the trees. Loomis has laid a trap.

He comes after her with Faro on the leash and a gun under his arm. Ann runs to the hollow tree and gets her gun. She moves north, reaching the banks of Burden Creek. She crosses on stepping stones and sights her rifle behind a rock. Loomis and Faro are following, and Faro leaps into the water. Loomis jerks back and Ann fires a shot above his head. Loomis had not known Ann had the gun. She fires again and Loomis heads back towards the house. Faro is swimming in the contaminated water. She leads the dog to her camp where she tries to feed him but he is not interested. In the morning he is sick, and by nightfall he is dead.

Ann is now ready to start her plan.

COMMENT   Ann's dream is linked to her desire to help others. The reader is left to wonder whether it is merely a dream based on her previous expectations, or perhaps a premonition of something that is to come about.

Ann displays uncharacteristic procrastination in putting her plan into action. She is perhaps lulled by Loomis's seeming reluctance to continue tracking her, and also by the fact that she knows he will kill to protect the safe-suit.

Even the sounds of nature now frighten Ann instead of giving her comfort.

It is Loomis's action of burning her last book which raises her desire for revenge. He has tried to rape her and to keep her prisoner and he has shot her, but even in these circumstances her deeply moral upbringing prevents her from expressing out-and-out hatred.

CHAPTER 25

August 7th

Ann is at the top of Burden Hill, wearing the safe-suit. She has wisely taken the cart and supplies out of the valley towards Ogdentown, but she has decided that she must come back to speak to Loomis. Ann realises the danger in this but she has a gun. She knows, however, that she could not kill him. She compares her offensive against Loomis to games of chess she once played with her father. She tells us how she put her plan into action.

Ann is now 'taking the offensive'.

Ann takes the gun, food, water and clothing down into the valley before dawn. Hiding her supplies in the ravine, she approaches the house. She has written a note which she leaves under a stone on the front porch. It asks Loomis to meet her at the south end of the valley, and to leave his gun behind.

She hides and watches as Loomis comes out. He reads the note in the house, and after a while, leaving his gun on the porch, he makes his way to the meeting place. Ann runs to get the cart, loaded with equipment, and pulls it up the road, passing the house. She remembers her past life there, but also tries to think of her dream. She thinks of Faro, and a tear comes to her eye, but she also remembers Loomis when he was ill, and the sadness she felt when she thought he was going to die.

Ann knows he will be enraged, and that he will do anything to make her stay. She puts her supplies into the wagon, puts on the safe-suit, and rolls the cart down hill towards Ogdentown. She comes back with the notebook and the gun and waits for Loomis.

COMMENT   Although we know from what she tells us at the start of this diary entry that Ann has the suit, the tension is sustained right until the final chapter, as we do not know what the result of her final confrontation with Loomis will be. The last sentence of the chapter heightens the suspense. Ann fatalistically writes: 'I am glad to have told my story' (p. 262). His may be the last human voice she hears.

Ann's courage and sense of what is right have never been in question, but here, in perhaps her most courageous act, she determines she will speak to Loomis one last time. Even now, she knows she cannot kill him.

Ann has referred to her struggle against Loomis as a game of chess once before in Chapter 20. Then it was his game, now she is on the offensive.

Her feelings of sadness at leaving are reflected in her memories as she pulls the cart out of the valley. We are made aware of the gigantic and dangerous step she is taking.

CHAPTER 26

August 8th   The plan seems to be going awry. Loomis approaches on the tractor at top speed with the gun. Ann shouts to him to stop, and fires her gun in the air, but he ignores her and brings the tractor to a halt opposite her hiding place. He jumps down, looking for her. He has his back to her but she cannot bring herself to shoot him. Ann calls on Loomis to drop his gun, but he wheels around and fires. She believes she is going to die after all her efforts to survive. Her disappointment is so great that it overcomes her fear, and she stands up to confront him.

Loomis does not shoot. When he sees the safe-suit he yells that it is his, and tells Ann to take it off. She refuses and he points the gun at her. Without thinking, Ann reveals to Loomis that she knows he killed Edward; she realises that telling him this probably saved her life. Loomis turns away and, trembling, says Edward tried to steal the suit, as Ann is doing now. Ann explains that she has no choice. She will not be hunted and she will not be held a prisoner.

Loomis's desperation is revealed.

Loomis pleads with her not to go, not to leave him alone. Ann tells Loomis that if he kills her he will really be alone. He has the valley. If she finds people she will tell them about him and they may come to find him. Her last words are that he did not even thank her for looking after him when he was ill, and she reflects that her last words are childish.

She turns her back on him and waits to be killed. But the shot never comes, and she walks away. He shouts after her, and she turns to see him standing on the edge of the deadness, pointing westwards, indicating where he has seen birds circling. Ann raises her hand in acknowledgement and walks away.

Ann leaves the valley in hope.

Ann has walked all afternoon and nearly all night. She has slept a little, not knowing where she is, but the dream has returned. In it she has found the schoolroom and the children. On waking, the sun is high and there is a stream flowing west. She walks on, hopeful, looking for a trace of green.

COMMENT

Ann is not infallible. She has made mistakes in the past, and now we see Loomis thundering after her with the gun – she could easily have taken this with her. Even now she will not shoot Loomis. Instead she is ready to die herself.

Why does Loomis allow Ann to go?

We are left to speculate as to why Ann's words about Edward make Loomis cave in. It may be that they confront him with his guilt; or that he sees a recurrence of the very same scenario and he cannot let it happen again; or that he realises Ann has known about this but still cared for him; or a combination of these.

Loomis breaks down and reveals himself as the frightened, guilty, weak person he is or has become. The reader perhaps begins to feel some sympathy for him, particularly when he makes one final gesture of goodwill by pointing out the birds, the **symbols** (see Literary Terms) of hope, to the west.

Ann recognises that she does feel bitter. Loomis now has everything that was once hers, but even more, he has rejected any chance they had of sharing them and forging a future together. He has gone about everything the wrong way, whereas Ann remains moral and correct to the end.

Although we do not know what happens to Ann, the shining sun and the optimistic dream ensure that the story ends with a feeling of hope.

Identify the speaker.

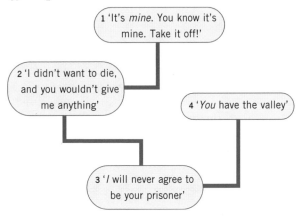

1 'It's *mine*. You know it's mine. Take it off!'

2 'I didn't want to die, and you wouldn't give me anything'

4 '*You* have the valley'

3 '*I* will never agree to be your prisoner'

Identify the person(s) 'to whom' this comment refers.

5 'a small and tidy woman'

6 'he missed his chance'

Check your answers on page 91.

B **Consider these issues.**

a Whether or not it is sensible of Ann to share the food and provisions so fairly with Loomis.

b The way in which Robert O'Brien uses time, moving backwards and forwards, and the way in which the diary form helps create suspense.

c Ann's inability to shoot the dog or Loomis.

d The use of dreams in the novel.

e To what extent the reader gains sympathy for Loomis as the novel draws to its close.

f The hope and optimism which is sensed at the end of the novel, and how it is brought about.

PART THREE

COMMENTARY

THEMES

The themes of *Z for Zachariah* are to do with the fundamental issues of what it is to be human. All human beings have, of course, good and bad within them. In this novel, due to the unique and desperate circumstances in which the characters find themselves, these opposites are highlighted. The fact that the two **protagonists** (see Literary Terms) are, as far as we and they know, the only two people left on earth, serves to throw their contrast into starker relief. The four themes discussed below are listed as opposites, but as in any good work of literature, the issues are complex and interlinked.

GOOD AND EVIL

Consider the parallels with the story of Genesis.

The title of the novel brings the reader to consider good and evil, innocence and experience. Ann tells us that she possessed a picture book called *The Bible Letter Book*, in which the letters of the alphabet were illustrated by characters from the Bible. It began with 'A is for Adam' and ended with 'Z is for Zachariah', and since Adam was the first man, she had assumed for a long time that Zachariah was the last man. A clear parallel can be drawn: Adam and Eve were the first man and woman, just as Loomis and Ann are the last. The Bible states that Adam and Eve lived in the Garden of Eden, in which grew 'every tree that is pleasant to the sight, and good for food … And a river went out of Eden to water the garden' (Genesis 2:9–10). The valley in *Z for Zachariah* can be compared to the Garden of Eden, a place where food and good water is available; outside is wilderness. When Eve, and then Adam, eat the fruit of the one tree God has forbidden them to touch – the Tree of Knowledge – God is angry. Adam is banished from the Garden, because 'the man is become as one of us, to know good and evil' (Genesis 3:22). In *Z for Zachariah*, Ann, at first, is innocent to a large extent. Loomis's arrival brings about a change, he brings about a contamination of the valley's peace and harmony, and, in the end, Ann must leave: 'I went into the deadness' (p. 266).

At the beginning of the novel we find the earth has been all but destroyed by forces Ann was obviously powerless to control, the evil use of scientific progress in the form of nuclear war. Ann, however, has risen above this. She tells us that her first reaction to the sight of smoke from Loomis's campfire has been to go to the church and pray all morning. The last time she had seen smoke outside the valley it has been the smoke of the nuclear war, the smoke of destruction.

Ann fears that the approaching stranger may be evil: 'suppose he was crazy? Or suppose it was someone mean, or even cruel, and brutal? A murderer?' (p. 10). These words are proven to be prophetically **ironic** (see Literary Terms); but this is not to say that the rest of the story is a clear-cut case of Ann representing good and Loomis representing evil. Ann certainly displays no trace of what we might in any way term evil. The nearest she comes to displaying any of the negative characteristics common to humanity is when at the end of the novel, having been forced to endure the most terrible ordeals at Loomis's hands, she tells us that although she is not sure whether she has ever hated anybody, she wanted to hurt Loomis, to 'cause him grief' (p. 247). She plans revenge, which she achieves by taking the safe-suit. She has travelled from innocence to experience.

In taking the safe-suit, is it fair to describe Ann's actions as 'stealing'?

We could speak of Loomis's 'inhuman' behaviour, but it would be truer to say that whereas Ann represents many of the good and positive features of human beings, Loomis displays many of the evil and negative characteristics. This is due, in large part, to the solidity of Ann's Christian upbringing: as a child she was taught that hatred was wrong.

Ann's goodness is not a totally naïve goodness. She has grown up surrounded by good people, in a loving and caring environment, which she remembers fondly in times of danger; but she has been brought up with discipline – she tells us that Faro used to crawl under the porch when she or Joseph or David were scolded – and, of course, she has lived through the horror of nuclear war. So it is reasonable that Ann is wary of Loomis and that she conceals herself in the cave when he appears in the valley.

Why are Loomis's violent actions so shocking?

Perhaps the first indication that Loomis is a violent person is when he shoots one of Ann's chickens. Ann finds violence and destruction shocking, but she is always ready to forgive and make excuses for Loomis's behaviour.

Ann's ambitions have always been to help people – 'I liked most people' she tells us – but she knows, from what she heard on the radio during the war, that people can be 'desperate and selfish' (p. 41). When Loomis is ill Ann cares for him and prays for him, even when she knows that he has probably murdered Edward. Ann tries as hard as she can to justify Loomis's actions, arguing that he killed Edward in self-defence, and even attempting to persuade herself that Loomis had not just been considering his own survival, but that of the entire human race. This fairness, this selflessness, is even more in evidence when Ann, despite having been nearly raped by Loomis, shares out the food and provisions so meticulously between herself and her attacker. She tries even then to compromise and to communicate. She has opportunities to shoot Loomis, to kill him. In the circumstances, many people might have been tempted to do just that, but Ann's strong sense of morality, of what is wrong and what is right, prevents her from doing so. She will not even kill Faro when the dog becomes a threat.

Loomis's behaviour is in total contrast to this. He kills as soon as he enters the valley. As he recovers from illness he becomes more and more selfish. He wants Ann as a possession, not as a companion, and he cynically begins to treat her as a slave, showing no gratitude for the care she has taken of him.

Do you regard Loomis as evil?

We can perhaps justify, if not condone, some of Loomis's behaviour. He has lived through unique and terrible events, but then so has Ann. He finds it difficult to behave in a caring and humanitarian way, resulting in his appalling treatment of Ann, and his attempt to rape her. He taunts Ann, he has no respect for her religious beliefs or her rights to individuality and freedom. When Ann tries to compromise, Loomis shoots her. He then attempts to track her down like a hunted animal. But are these the actions of an evil man, or a man, as Ann recognises later in the novel, who is sad, lonely and frightened? Loomis displays traits which can be described as evil, but, in the end, he does not kill her when he has the chance. Instead, he points her to where he has seen signs of life, and he gains something of the Christian ideal of redemption.

LIFE AND DEATH

At the beginning of the novel, Ann believes that she is the only human being alive. There is life inside the valley, and only deadness outside. Loomis comes from outside the valley and brings death and destruction with him, just as Burden Creek comes from outside the valley and kills everything it touches.

Ann nurtures the plants and animals of the valley in order to create new life and, therefore, to continue nature's existence. The continuation of the human race depends, of course, on the arrival of a man, to promulgate the species. The arrival of Loomis should therefore be a cause of great hope and celebration. Ann has hopes of 'marrying' Loomis and having children; Loomis sees the importance of founding a 'colony'. The difference between these two concepts is important, as Ann's idea includes the belief that some sort of spiritual bonding is necessary, not just a physical union.

Ann has respect for all forms of life, demonstrated, for example, when she saves the baby crow. Her upbringing on the farm has made her practical enough to allow her to fish and to kill chickens for food, but she is unable to shoot Faro, even when it seems certain that the dog will lead Loomis to her hiding place. She has only shot at bottles and cans, whereas Loomis shoots a chicken as one of his first actions in the valley. Ann cannot bring herself to shoot Loomis; that would be against her moral code. Instead, she leaves the valley, in the hope that life exists elsewhere, and with the promise that if she can she will send people to help Loomis.

HOPE AND DESPAIR

In her days of loneliness, Ann had hoped that someone would come to the valley. However, when a sign of life does appear, she is afraid. Despite her reservations, Ann starts to entertain thoughts of marriage and children with Loomis, and at this point the future looks promising.

Optimism   Ann is naturally optimistic, strengthened by her faith in God and her positive upbringing. Her hopes often become fact: Loomis recovers; the stove works again; the tractor can be used. Ann sees **symbols** (see Literary Terms) of hope in the natural world: the apple blossom is a symbol of her hope of marriage to Loomis, but later it withers and dies, representing the death of this ambition. Saving the baby crow gives her a sense of hope and optimism for the future.

Dreams

Ann's dreams, too, provide her with a sense of purpose. We believe with her that there may be, somewhere out there, in another valley, living human beings, a class of schoolchildren waiting for their teacher.

The final words of the novel are 'I am hopeful' (p. 267) and our hopes are not just for Ann, but for the continuation of the human race. We are also left with hope, in as much as Loomis has at last shown some of the positive characteristics of mankind, directing her towards life, towards the west, where the birds fly.

ART AND SCIENCE

Z for Zachariah may be classified as a science-fiction novel. Loomis is a scientist, but because of the **first-person narrative** (see Literary Terms) any scientific details are recounted through the words of Ann, who is not a scientist, although she is interested in science. Understanding is thus made easy, and any disbelief we may experience as to, for example, the possibility of a valley remaining uncontaminated by nuclear fallout, is made secondary by the drive of the narrative.

Would the situation make for as interesting a story if their partnership was successful?

Often in the story we are made to think 'if only ...'. If only Loomis's scientific knowledge and logical mind had been allowed to combine with Ann's practical farming knowledge, common sense and sensibility, this would surely have been a fortuitous, formidable and positive relationship. Ann is practical and able, skilled in the ways of farming, having helped and watched her father. She is also sensitive, spiritual and artistic. She believes in God and the power of prayer. She loves literature and music, which she uses in bringing Loomis back to health. Loomis, on the other hand, sneers at Ann's church-going, and sees it as a waste of time. He is seemingly insensitive to the beauty of nature. He is also oblivious to the need for literature, and believes that the only useful books are 'practical' ones. Science, of course, is practical. Loomis has worked on the development of the plastic which has resulted in the production of the safe-suit. Had it been produced earlier, the future of the human race might have been much more secure. Loomis is able to make the petrol pumps work again and he plans to build a dam in order to restore some electricity to the valley. His obsession with control, however, leads him to be insensitive, cruel, and unable to communicate in any caring and cooperative manner.

The fact that he at first truly enjoys Ann's reading and piano-playing shows that, perhaps unconsciously, he needs these things. When he burns the *Famous Short Stories of England and America*, Ann finally decides to leave the valley. The combination of Ann and Loomis's positive characteristics could have provided a firm base for the future of the human race, but the relationship founders on Loomis's self-centredness.

STRUCTURE

Z for Zachariah is written in the form of a diary, and the action of the novel is therefore recounted as a **first-person narrative** (see Literary Terms) by Ann Burden, everything being seen through her eyes and from her point of view. The diary entries start on May 20th of an unspecified year sometime in the future, and end on

August 8th in the same year. On one level, this is a very false device: how can we be reading the diary of events that will happen in the future, after some as yet to be experienced nuclear war? On a practical level, this reservation does not really arise. In reading the novel the reader enters into what the poet and critic Samuel Taylor Coleridge called 'the willing suspension of disbelief'. We are pulled along by the strength of the narrative, and any questioning of the total logic of the piece is almost irrelevant. The reader forgets that this is a very carefully constructed novel by Robert O'Brien – we choose to believe it is a diary written by teenager Ann Burden.

The diary form allows Ann not just to tell us what happens on each particular day, but to recount what has happened in the past. This is useful for the **exposition** (see Literary Terms) at the beginning of the novel, when we must learn the background of the nuclear war and Ann's previous life with her family in the valley.

Flashbacks   Robert O'Brien's use of time is extremely clever. Throughout the novel, **flashbacks** (see Literary Terms) are used in subtle and effective ways. Ann frequently refers back to times before the war with her family, and she hears Loomis, both consciously and unconsciously, describe what happened in his life before he entered the valley. As well as these references to events prior to the start of the diary, there are also flashbacks within the timescale of the diary, when Ann has been unable or unwilling to write for a day or more, and she has to tell us what has happened since her last diary entry.

This leads us to the use of **hooklines** (see Literary Terms), which the author uses throughout the novel in order to keep the reader in suspense. The very first sentence of the novel is an example: 'I am afraid' (p. 5). Robert O'Brien continues this device with page-turning regularity, for example: 'Now it is night. He is in my house' (p. 24); 'I am in terrible trouble. Mr Loomis *shot* me' (p 211). On these occasions the reader is drawn into the narrative, as Ann tells the reader what has happened in the lead-up to each event. We are in suspense as to what has occurred.

Suspense and tension

Suspense and tension are formidable qualities of the novel. We really want to know what happens to Ann. But seeing the events through Ann's eyes only serves to heighten the tension, as we can never be sure what Mr Loomis is thinking. We are with Ann all of the time, we side with her, and we also worry and fear with her.

The **first-person narrative** (see Literary Terms) creates uncertainty and ambiguity. If the story were told in the third person by an all-seeing narrator, the reader might know, for example, who the approaching stranger is and what Loomis's plans and motivations are. In many ways, it is more exciting and more 'real' when we do not know. For example, when Loomis drops his stick, we are no more knowledgeable than Ann as to whether it was done on purpose or if it was an accident.

Prophecies

Throughout the novel, linked to the idea of dreams and premonitions, Ann is aware of dangers which later become prophetically true. Will Loomis be mad, or bad, or cruel? He becomes so. Will Faro give Ann away? He nearly does. Might Loomis make her his slave? He tries to.

The first words of the novel are 'I am afraid', the last words are 'I am hopeful'. There is a sense of an almost religious journey about the progress of the novel; the Bible tells us the greatest sin is despair, and Ann never succumbs to this, despite all that happens to her.

CHARACTERS

ANN BURDEN

Practical
Caring
Optimistic
Sensitive

Ann Burden, at the beginning of the novel, is fifteen years of age, and she believes she is the only person left alive in the world. This is an extraordinary situation in which to find oneself at any age, and how she copes when a man appears in her valley and threatens her existence is the essence of the story.

Ann has lived through a nuclear war. Her parents and brother and cousin have all gone off, looking for life, and they have never returned. She has been alone for over a year, having heard grown men break down on the radio and having decided that outside the valley is just deadness. Many people might have given in to despair, fallen apart, and given up on life. But Ann Burden, as we come to find out, is an extraordinary human being, one who **symbolises** (see Literary Terms) the spirit and hope, the positive virtues of humanity. Far from giving up, she has used the farming knowledge, common sense and practicality with which her upbringing has provided her. She has created for herself a haven of life in the middle of the wilderness, living a dignified and hopeful existence.

When she spies a stranger approaching she does not immediately reveal her presence. She is careful, prudent and wise beyond her years. She knows men can be cruel as well as kind. She is sensible enough to be able to give up her almost cosy existence, dig up her vegetable garden and hide in the cave when the stranger enters the valley, so as to allow herself time to judge the motivations and character of the newcomer.

In appearance we know she is skinny, but 'not as skinny as I used to be' (p. 22). She keeps her hair cut off straight around the neck and she keeps it clean. She retains her dignity and dresses in a practical way, using the clothes available to her from the store.

Ann's behaviour does represent all the good and
decent traits of humankind, the characteristics which
perhaps set us apart from animals. Her upbringing
has ensured this. Ann has a spiritual and emotional
depth which is truly admirable. She prays, and visits
the church; she enjoys playing the piano, especially
hymns. When there was a future outside the valley she
had considered becoming a nurse or a teacher. She
genuinely cares for people and wants to help them.

She becomes a nurse in an unforeseen way when
Loomis becomes ill. She takes excellent care of him,
working out what to do with a combination of
experience and common sense. Despite starting to
suspect that Loomis is a murderer, she continues
to care for him. She retains the Christian values of
hope and forgiveness, and attempts to understand and
justify his actions. She always thinks things through
logically and methodically, whether it be the planting
of the crops, the husbandry of the animals, or the
reasons behind Loomis's shooting of Edward.

Ann has a deep respect for life. She is not against the
killing of animals for food, but when she contemplates
shooting Faro so as to secure her own safety, she cannot
pull the trigger – she considers herself to be a murderer
for even thinking about such an action. When she has
the chance to kill Loomis, she would rather die herself
than do so.

Ann finds optimism in nature. As she is ploughing, she
feels like singing. She recites poetry to herself, and
watches crows in the sky. She finds apple blossom and
dreams of a marriage to Loomis.

She dreams of having children, but all this comes to
nothing as Loomis's behaviour becomes more and more
tyrannical. Even when Loomis's desire for domination
becomes intolerable, even when he has attempted to
rape her and control her, Ann's morality does not come

into question. She still feels a responsibility towards his well-being, meticulously sharing the food and provisions.

Ann knows the value of communication. She tries to talk to Loomis, to compromise with him, and he shoots her. He tries to destroy, whereas she tries to create. Even when she knows she must leave the valley and takes the suit, she feels the need to speak to Loomis one last time.

Note the number of times Ann refers to 'Poor Mr Loomis' or 'Poor Faro'.

Despite all this, the reader never thinks Ann is too good to be true. She is strong, moral and sympathetic, but Robert O'Brien succeeds in making Ann Burden a rounded character. Her surname is perhaps **symbolic** (see Literary Terms): she has many burdens to bear, and she bears them stoically. She has incredible self-control, and whenever her thoughts turn to her dead family, she strains desperately to put them out of her mind. At the end of the novel she feels she wants to hurt Loomis and she wants revenge. We have to be reminded that she is still a child, and she recognises that her last words to him are childish: 'You didn't even thank me for taking care of you when you were ill' (p. 265).

It is Ann's dreams which finally lead her out of the valley – the thought that somewhere there is another valley, with children waiting to be taught. If she finds people, she will send them for Loomis, but she cannot live with him. Ann is able to believe in dreams, and the reader is able to believe that if she finds another valley, the continuation of the human race will be in good hands if she is part of its future.

JOHN R. LOOMIS

Loomis brings death and destruction to the valley, and Ann is right to be cautious of him as he approaches.

Selfish
Violent
Reckless
Scientific

Physically he is quite attractive to Ann. When he trims his hair and beard Ann comments that 'he looks almost handsome' (p. 42). His face is long and narrow, and he has quite a big nose. He is in his early thirties.

From the start Loomis behaves in a wary manner. At first he does not sleep in the house, but this caution is understandable. It is also understandable that he should make use of what the valley provides in the way of food and resources, although the reader perhaps shares Ann's feelings of slight indignation that he should shoot her chicken. It is his manner of killing the chicken, more than anything, which shocks Ann. It is over-violent, and almost desperate – characteristics we see in Loomis to a larger extent later on.

Ann's fears about the stranger are renewed by his indiscriminate shooting at something – a rabbit? – in the bushes, but then we feel concern for him when he takes his reckless leap into Burden Creek. Despite Loomis's supposition of his own superiority later in the novel, we are shown by this big mistake that Loomis can be wrong, he can be careless; he is not infallible.

We find out that Loomis is a scientist, and that he must have been well respected to be invited to work with a Nobel prizewinner. Loomis's scientific knowledge has helped in the development of the safe-suit, which could have proved to be the salvation of the human race had it been mass-produced. His technical knowledge allows him to get the petrol pumps working again, and he makes plans to generate electricity using water power. If Loomis's scientific skills had been used in cooperation with Ann, their alliance may well have been successful and happy. However, Ann begins to realise that there is something sinister in Loomis's background, and when we find out that he is a murderer we start to see that this man could never be a compatible companion for the sensitive and moral Ann.

Ann attempts to justify Loomis's murder of Edward. There is some logic in her argument that he may have been acting for the benefit of the world as a whole, but in the light of Loomis's totally selfish behaviour towards Ann later, this seems unlikely. As Loomis becomes well again, he becomes overbearing and domineering to the level of tyranny.

Just as the author lets us appreciate Ann as a rounded individual, we cannot be allowed to look on Loomis as merely the evil force which descends on the valley. When Ann asks him if he wants her to play the piano, he is extremely enthusiastic. When she has finished, he tells her 'This is the best evening I have ever spent' (p. 81). Loomis reveals his vulnerability when Ann asks him if he means his best night since the war. He spoils the atmosphere by responding angrily, 'You heard me … I said "ever"' (p. 81). Loomis states that he comes from a poor background, but it is evident that his background has been spiritually, emotionally and culturally deprived; he has not just been poor in material terms.

Loomis attaches no importance to Ann's artistic and spiritual needs

Thus when Ann suggests using the suit to go to Ogdentown for books, Loomis asserts that the suit cannot be risked for such a trivial purpose. He cannot see the importance of the arts, nor can he recognise Ann's need for some spiritual dimension in her life. He mocks her church-going and praying, and he has no real respect for the natural world or any life other than his own. To broaden the picture, he is representative of the society which can allow itself to be destroyed by nuclear weapons and nerve gas, a **symbol** (see Literary Terms) of the contemporary man.

Loomis cannot cope with the awful predicament in which he finds himself. He lacks Ann's inner resources. However, it is difficult to make any excuse for his attempt to rape Ann, or his later attempt to shoot her.

He refuses or is unable to see her goodness in caring for him when he was ill and bringing him provisions when she was living in the cave. Loomis tries to possess and rule Ann; when she hides in the cave he tries to hunt her down; and when this fails he tries to starve her into submission.

When Ann plays Loomis at his own game and takes the safe-suit, Loomis reveals himself to be 'frightened and bewildered' (p. 265). His penultimate words betray his desperation: 'Don't go … Don't leave me here alone' (p. 265). Loomis's final words, however, give the reader hope that he is heading towards some sort of salvation. He indicates the birds to the west, a gesture at odds with the selfishness he has displayed up until now. We do not know why he does this but perhaps some of Ann's goodness and selflessness has rubbed off on Loomis, just as he brought spiritual contamination to the valley.

FARO

Compare Loomis's treatment of Faro to his treatment of Ann.

Faro was Ann's cousin David's dog. He returns to the house soon after Loomis's arrival, having gone missing, presumably in search of David, when the rest of the family left the valley. When he comes back he is in a very bad condition, thin, and with half the hair gone from his left side.

At first Faro is wary of Loomis, just like Ann, but Loomis feeds him chicken to win his confidence. Then Faro picks up Ann's trail and follows it to the cave. Ann fears that the dog will give her away, a concern that later proves to be well founded.

Loomis keeps Faro prisoner, tied up with an electric cable that the dog cannot chew through. Then he uses Faro to track Ann and to try to find her hiding place in the cave. Faro has previously saved Ann from Loomis's attempted rape, by barking as Loomis approached the bed. And the dog has accompanied Ann around the farm and on her visits to the church. It is these attachments, together with Ann's respect for life, which prevent her from shooting Faro when the dog is a real source of danger to her.

Faro later dies by leaping into the contaminated stream, and this prompts Ann to put her plan for leaving the valley into action.

MINOR CHARACTERS – THE DEAD

Ann's family   Those people who have died are important to the background of the story. Ann's father and mother have provided her with the upbringing which allows her to be able to survive both physically and mentally in the desperate situations in which she finds herself. Obviously stoical and moral, they brought up Ann, her brother Joseph and her cousin David, who had moved in about five years before when his father had died, leaving him an orphan. Ann's parents taught her practical skills and imbued her with a strong sense of right and wrong, a love of the arts and nature, and common sense.

The Kleins   The Kleins, who ran the store, have left Ann an important source of food, provisions and clothing. Ann has only once ventured, guiltily, into their living quarters, in search of books. But she found none, only a sense of a clean and well-ordered household that perhaps too had suffered loss, judging from the photograph of a son or brother which was lying on the bed, probably the last thing they had looked at before venturing out of the valley to their own deaths.

Edward   Edward's situation has been a foretaste of Ann's. He too wanted the suit, he too faced Loomis's desire for control, and he too faced Loomis's gun; but Edward, unlike Ann, dies as a result of this.

Notice how the narrative style adapts itself to the action being described.

As the novel takes the form of the diary of a teenager, it would be unconvincing if it were written in a high literary style. Robert O'Brien does well to make Ann's journal completely believable, and the **hooklines** and **flashbacks** (see Literary Terms), far from seeming unnatural, seem totally realistic.

There is, therefore, no extensive use of metaphor or simile, but certain things and objects do take on a **symbolic** (see Literary Terms) meaning. Birds are an obvious example. Ann states that she has always thoughts that birds bring good luck, and she actually tells us on page 135 that she sees them as symbols of optimism. Thus when she finds the baby crow she sees it as a good omen; when the war began the birds disappeared; and at the end of the novel Loomis points out that he has seen birds to the west, indicating hope for Ann's journey. The crabapple tree and the apple blossom are also used symbolically. At first, Ann sees the crabapple tree in full bloom, another sign of hope which brings about thoughts of marriage. She takes some of the blossom into the house and places it in Loomis's bedroom, but later it dies, as do Ann's hopes of a future with Loomis. The apple blossom is sweet-smelling but its fruit is sour.

Ann's love of nature is reflected in her writing.

There is symbolism too in other aspects of nature, such as the contrast of the green of the valley with the wilderness outside, and the two streams, one bringing poison into the valley from outside, as Loomis in a sense does, the other emanating from within the valley, good and pure like Ann. Many objects take on a symbolic significance, for example the guns representing Loomis's violence.

Description in *Z for Zachariah* follows on from Ann's desire to explain. Overall, the style of the novel is matter-of-fact and in some ways understated, underlining Ann's common sense and practicality.

Part four

Study skills

How to use quotations

One of the secrets of success in writing essays is the way you use quotations. There are five basic principles:

- Put inverted commas at the beginning and end of the quotation
- Write the quotation exactly as it appears in the original
- Do not use a quotation that repeats what you have just written
- Use the quotation so that it fits into your sentence
- Keep the quotation as short as possible

Quotations should be used to develop the line of thought in your essays. Your comment should not duplicate what is in your quotation. For example:

Ann thinks that by tapping his stick, Loomis is trying to frighten her: 'maybe he is trying to frighten me'.

Far more effective is to write:

When Loomis taps his stick, Ann thinks 'maybe he is trying to frighten me'.

The most sophisticated way of using the writer's words is to embed them into your sentence:

When Ann confronts Loomis for the final time, the reader realises, with her, that he has become 'frightened and bewildered'.

When you use quotations in this way, you are demonstrating the ability to use text as evidence to support your ideas - not simply including words from the original to prove you have read it.

Everyone writes differently. Work through the suggestions given here and adapt the advice to suit your own style and interests. This will improve your essay-writing skills and allow your personal voice to emerge.

The following points indicate in ascending order the skills of essay writing:

- Picking out one or two facts about the story and adding the odd detail
- Writing about the text by retelling the story
- Retelling the story and adding a quotation here and there
- Organising an answer which explains what is happening in the text and giving quotations to support what you write

....

- Writing in such a way as to show that you have thought about the intentions of the writer of the text and that you understand the techniques used
- Writing at some length, giving your viewpoint on the text and commenting by picking out details to support your views
- Looking at the text as a work of art, demonstrating clear critical judgement and explaining to the reader of your essay how the enjoyment of the text is assisted by literary devices, linguistic effects and psychological insights; showing how the text relates to the time when it was written

The dotted line above represents the division between lower and higher level grades. Higher-level performance begins when you start to consider your response as a reader of the text. The highest level is reached when you offer an enthusiastic personal response and show how this piece of literature is a product of its time.

Coursework Set aside an hour or so at the start of your work to plan
essay   what you have to do.

- List all the points you feel are needed to cover the task. Collect page references of information and quotations that will support what you have to say. A helpful tool is the highlighter pen: this saves painstaking copying and enables you to target precisely what you want to use.
- Focus on what you consider to be the main points of the essay. Try to sum up your argument in a single sentence, which could be the closing sentence of your essay. Depending on the essay title, it could be a statement about a character: Ann's morality, practicality and fairness have helped her to survive, and these qualities give us hope for the survival of the human race; an opinion about setting: Burden Valley is like a Garden of Eden, set amidst the wilderness, but it is tainted by the outside world and so Ann must leave; or a judgement on a theme: An important theme of *Z for Zachariah* is the struggle between good and evil which goes on within all human beings, but it is too simplistic to say that Ann is totally good and Loomis totally evil.
- Make a short essay plan. Use the first paragraph to introduce the argument you wish to make. In the following paragraphs develop this argument with details, examples and other possible points of view. Sum up your argument in the last paragraph. Check you have answered the question.
- Write the essay, remembering all the time the central point you are making.
- On completion, go back over what you have written to eliminate careless errors and improve expression. Read it aloud to yourself, or, if you are feeling more confident, to a relative or friend.

If you can, try to type your essay using a word processor. This will allow you to correct and improve your writing without spoiling its appearance.

*Examination
essay*

The essay written in an examination often carries more marks than the coursework essay even though it is written under considerable time pressure.

In the revision period build up notes on various aspects of the text you are using. Fortunately, in acquiring this set of York Notes on *Z for Zachariah*, you have made a prudent beginning! York Notes are set out to give you vital information and help you to construct your personal overview of the text.

Make notes with appropriate quotations about the key issues of the set text. Go into the examination knowing your text and having a clear set of opinions about it.

*In the
examination*

In most English Literature examinations you can take in copies of your set books. This is an enormous advantage although it may lull you into a false sense of security. Beware! There is simply not enough time in an examination to read the book from scratch.

- Read the question paper carefully and remind yourself what you have to do
- Look at the questions on your set texts to select the one that most interests you and mentally work out the points you wish to stress
- Remind yourself of the time available and how you are going to use it
- Briefly map out a short plan in note form that will keep your writing on track and illustrate the key argument you want to make.
- Then set about writing it
- When you have finished, check through to eliminate errors

*To summarise,
these are keys
to success*

- **Know the text**
- **Have a clear understanding of and opinions on the storyline, characters, setting, themes and writer's concerns**
- **Select the right material**
- **Plan and write a clear response, continually bearing the question in mind**

SAMPLE ESSAY PLAN

A typical essay question on *Z for Zachariah* is followed by a sample essay plan in note form. This does not present the only answer to the question, so do not be afraid to include your own ideas, or exclude some of the following. Remember that quotations are essential to prove and illustrate the points you make.

Consider how the themes of life and death are relevant to an understanding of *Z for Zachariah*.

Introduction Life and death are essential elements in the novel. The war has caused death. As far as Ann knows she is the only person left alive on earth – until Loomis appears. Ann's struggle for life has been successful up until Loomis's arrival. After he arrives it soon becomes a struggle not against the effects of the war, but against him.

Part 1 Ann by herself.
- Ann has coped exceptionally well in harrowing circumstances.
- She has survived but her family have died, as have the Kleins, the Amish, the people on the radio, probably everyone in the world. Although sad, Ann has coped mentally, through her toughness of spirit and practicality.
- The valley has survived, allowing Ann to eat fresh food, drink fresh water, and make use of the provisions in the store.

Part 2 Loomis arrives.
- Just as Burden Creek brings poison into the valley and destroys all it touches, Loomis comes from outside the valley and brings violence and death.
- He seems careless with life; uses his gun in a reckless manner. Then he is careless with his own life and comes near death because of his bath in the polluted stream.

- Ann respects all life and does what she can to preserve it (e.g. nursing Loomis, saving the baby crow, tending to crops and animals). When she considers killing Faro she brands herself a murderer because of the very thought.
- We find out that Loomis is a murderer; he puts his life before all others. He envisages the foundation of a 'colony' whereas Ann hoped for 'marriage'.
- He enslaves Faro and tries to enslave Ann. He attempts to rape Ann and shoots her. He tries to starve her into submission even when she has shared everything with him.
- Ann cannot bring herself to kill Loomis when she has the chance. Loomis points Ann towards signs of life, and Ann walks off through the wasteland.

Part 3   Spiritual life.
- Part of what divides us from the animals is our ability to appreciate the spiritual and aesthetic. Ann has this quality whereas Loomis appears not to − e.g. sneers at her love of church and prayer; uses Ann's love of music and reading to try to entrap her.
- Ann's dreams of life in some other valley give her the courage to leave the life of the valley and venture out into the deadness.
- Loomis's change of attitude at the end gives us hope of life in the future; but mainly we rely on Ann to be fundamental to the survival of humankind.

Conclusion   Despite the war and the deaths of all those close to her, Ann is able to survive. She possesses life-affirming qualities. Loomis presents many of the negative traits of human beings, but, at the end of the novel, through his contact with Ann he begins to show signs of positive behaviour.

When Ann leaves the valley, she walks westward looking for life, and this gives hope to the reader for the survival of the human race.

1 To what extent does the environment play a part in the story of *Z for Zachariah*?

2 The final words of the novel are 'I am hopeful'. What has Ann to be hopeful about?

3 How much do the backgrounds of Ann and Loomis play a part in their ability to cope with the unique circumstances in which they find themselves?

4 What is the significance of the title *Z for Zachariah*?

5 What do you think are the main differences between Ann Burden and John Loomis?

6 Imagine that Loomis kept a diary from the time Ann left the house following his attempt to rape her. Write his diary entries from this point to the time after Ann has left the valley.

7 Ann Burden has an artistic nature; John Loomis's career has been rooted in science. How could these differences have been helpful to them if they had been able to live together in harmony? Why do you think it goes wrong?

8 How does the diary format affect your view of the characters and events in the novel?

9 What part do dreams play in *Z for Zachariah*?

10 Write about violence in *Z for Zachariah*.

11 What part do animals and birds play in *Z for Zachariah*?

12 What is your opinion of Loomis?

PART FIVE

CULTURAL CONNECTIONS

BROADER PERSPECTIVES

As an example of the science-fiction genre, *Z for Zachariah* (1974) may be compared with works by H.G. Wells, such as *The War of the Worlds* (1898) or *The Time Machine*, (1895) and glimpses into what may happen to the human race in the future are contained in novels such as *Nineteen Eighty-four* (1949) by George Orwell and *Brave New World* (1932) by Aldous Huxley. Ray Bradbury's *Fahrenheit 451* (1953) is set in a future in which books have been banned and teams of 'firemen' are sent out to burn any books they find.

When the Wind Blows (1982), a cartoon book by Raymond Briggs, looks at the consequences of nuclear war. You may be able to watch the documentary-style television play *Threads* (1983) by Barry Hines, based on the idea of a world-wide nuclear conflict.

The idea of Ann and Loomis living in an isolated, self-sufficient environment is one which finds echoes in many other stories. A starting point is the story of Adam and Eve in the Book of Genesis in the Bible, but other links are with stories set on islands, where self-sufficiency is all-important. Daniel Defoe's *Robinson Crusoe* (1719), R.M. Ballantyne's *The Coral Island* (1857) and William Golding's *Lord of the Flies* (1954) could be compared in many ways with *Z for Zachariah*.

black humour a cynical humour used despairingly in unpleasant situations

exposition the explanatory part at the beginning of a novel or play, where background information has to be passed on to the reader

first-person narrative a story told from the point of view of an 'I' character, like Ann Burden

flashbacks a jump backwards in time to fill in details which have occurred previously – a device frequently used in films, and now common in novels and plays

hookline a line, often at the beginning of a book or chapter, which 'grabs' the reader and makes him or her anxious to read on and find out what happens

irony saying one thing and meaning another – often through understatement concealment or indirect statement

motif a literary device, such as a theme, image or symbol, which recurs frequently, either throughout a body of literature or within a single work

protagonist the principal character in a story or play

symbolism the use of an object or idea to represent something else by association. For example, birds in *Z for Zachariah* can be seen as symbols of hope

TEST ANSWERS

TEST YOURSELF (Chapters 1–5)

A 1 Ann's mother *(Chapter 1)*
2 Ann's father *(Chapter 1)*
3 Loomis *(Chapter 3)*
4 Loomis *(Chapter 5)*
5 Loomis *(Chapter 5)*
6 Ann *(Chapter 1)*
7 Ann's father *(Chapter 1)*
8 Loomis *(Chapter 3)*

TEST YOURSELF (Chapters 6–10)

A 1 Loomis *(Chapter 6)*
2 Loomis *(Chapter 7)*
3 Ann *(Chapter 8)*
4 Loomis *(Chapter 10)*
5 Loomis *(Chapter 6)*
6 Ann's parents *(Chapter 6)*

TEST YOURSELF (Chapters 11–15)

A 1 Loomis *(Chapter 11)*
2 Loomis *(Chapter 11)*

3 Loomis *(Chapter 11)*
4 Ann *(Chapter 14)*
5 Loomis *(Chapter 14)*
6 Edward *(Chapter 11)*
7 Loomis *(Chapter 12)*

TEST YOURSELF (Chapters 16–20)

A 1 Loomis *(Chapter 16)*
2 Loomis *(Chapter 17)*
3 Loomis *(Chapter 20)*
4 Loomis *(Chapter 20)*
5 Loomis *(Chapter 20)*
6 Ann *(Chapter 20)*

TEST YOURSELF (Chapters 21–26)

A 1 Loomis *(Chapter 26)*
2 Ann *(Chapter 26)*
3 Ann *(Chapter 26)*
4 Ann *(Chapter 26)*
5 Mrs Klein *(Chapter 22)*
6 Loomis *(Chapter 24)*

Notes

GCSE and equivalent levels (£3.50 each)

Maya Angelou
I Know Why the Caged Bird Sings

Jane Austen
Pride and Prejudice

Harold Brighouse
Hobson's Choice

Charlotte Brontë
Jane Eyre

Emily Brontë
Wuthering Heights

Charles Dickens
David Copperfield

Charles Dickens
Great Expectations

Charles Dickens
Hard Times

George Eliot
Silas Marner

William Golding
Lord of the Flies

Willis Hall
The Long and the Short and the Tall

Thomas Hardy
Far from the Madding Crowd

Thomas Hardy
The Mayor of Casterbridge

Thomas Hardy
Tess of the d'Urbervilles

L.P. Hartley
The Go-Between

Seamus Heaney
Selected Poems

Susan Hill
I'm the King of the Castle

Barry Hines
A Kestrel for a Knave

Louise Lawrence
Children of the Dust

Harper Lee
To Kill a Mockingbird

Laurie Lee
Cider with Rosie

Arthur Miller
A View from the Bridge

Arthur Miller
The Crucible

Robert O'Brien
Z for Zachariah

George Orwell
Animal Farm

J.B. Priestley
An Inspector Calls

Willy Russell
Educating Rita

Willy Russell
Our Day Out

J.D. Salinger
The Catcher in the Rye

William Shakespeare
Henry V

William Shakespeare
Julius Caesar

William Shakespeare
Macbeth

William Shakespeare
A Midsummer Night's Dream

William Shakespeare
The Merchant of Venice

William Shakespeare
Romeo and Juliet

William Shakespeare
The Tempest

William Shakespeare
Twelfth Night

George Bernard Shaw
Pygmalion

R.C. Sherriff
Journey's End

Rukshana Smith
Salt on the snow

John Steinbeck
Of Mice and Men

R.L. Stevenson
Dr Jekyll and Mr Hyde

Robert Swindells
Daz 4 Zoe

Mildred D. Taylor
Roll of Thunder, Hear My Cry

Mark Twain
The Adventures of Huckleberry Finn

James Watson
Talking in Whispers

A Choice of Poets

Nineteenth Century Short Stories

Poetry of the First World War

Six Women Poets

Advanced level (£3.99 each)

Margaret Atwood
The Handmaid's Tale

William Blake
Songs of Innocence and of Experience

Emily Brontë
Wuthering Heights

Geoffrey Chaucer
The Wife of Bath's Prologue and Tale

Joseph Conrad
Heart of Darkness

Charles Dickens
Great Expectations

F. Scott Fitzgerald
The Great Gatsby

Thomas Hardy
Tess of the d'Urbervilles

James Joyce
Dubliners

Arthur Miller
Death of a Salesman

William Shakespeare
Antony and Cleopatra

William Shakespeare
Hamlet

William Shakespeare
King Lear

William Shakespeare
The Merchant of Venice

William Shakespeare
Romeo and Juliet

William Shakespeare
The Tempest

Mary Shelley
Frankenstein

Alice Walker
The Color Purple

Tennessee Williams
A Streetcar Named Desire

FORTHCOMING TITLES IN THE SERIES

Jane Austen
Emma

Jane Austen
Pride and Prejudice

Charlotte Brontë
Jane Eyre

Seamus Heaney
Selected Poems

William Shakespeare
Much Ado About Nothing

William Shakespeare
Othello

John Webster
The Duchess of Malfi